IMAGES
of America

TULSA'S KAKC RADIO
THE BIG 97

In the 1960s, KAKC'S Top 50 record survey was available in stores throughout the Tulsa area. It contained a list of the week's most popular songs and photographs of the Big 7 deejays, many of whom were celebrities in the community. This one is from March 28, 1966. Picking up this survey was a weekly ritual for many listeners of the New KAKC. (Courtesy of Wayne McCombs.)

On the Cover: Dick Clark introduces the Big 7 deejays on the Tulsa Civic Assembly Center stage in 1964. When the state-of-the-art 9,000-seat venue opened the previous year, Tulsa became a destination for rock-and-roll tours. KAKC sponsored many of those shows, including this sold-out Dick Clark's Cavalcade of Stars concert. Pictured are, from left to right, Harry Wilson, Gene Thomas, Dick Clark, Dick Ralston, Scooter Segraves, and Dick Schmitz. (Courtesy of Dick Schmitz.)

IMAGES
of America

Tulsa's KAKC Radio
The Big 97

Steve Clem

ARCADIA
PUBLISHING

ISBN 978-0-7385-9085-1

Published by Arcadia Publishing
Charleston, South Carolina

Printed in the United States of America

Library of Congress Control Number: 2012950209

For all general information, please contact Arcadia Publishing:
Telephone 843-853-2070
Fax 843-853-0044
E-mail sales@arcadiapublishing.com
For customer service and orders:
Toll-Free 1-888-313-2665

Visit us on the Internet at www.arcadiapublishing.com

This book is dedicated to Scooter Segraves and the others at KAKC who all made radio worth remembering. And to my parents, Jim and Rosa Lee Clem, for nurturing my radio dreams.

Contents

ACKNOWLEDGMENTS

I would like to extend a special note of gratitude to everyone who shared their photographs, memorabilia, and stories, which make up the contents of this book.

I conducted over 25 hours of original interviews with former KAKC personnel, and to them I extend many thanks. I am particularly grateful to Scooter Segraves, Dick Schmitz, Harry Wilson, Clayton Vaughn, Mike McCarthy, and Lee Bayley, who spent many hours answering my questions and poring over images. Also, to Bob Brown, Gary "Ono" Stevens, Robert Walker, Beau Weaver, Jim Peters, Steve Suttle, John Durkee, Randy Brown (a.k.a. "Bob Scott"), Chris Martin, Frank Morrow, and Johnny Mann—thank you all for sharing your history with me and for being as amazing as I remember you.

To the family of KAKC owner S. Carl Mark—Mary Alice (Mark) Alexander, Jon Mark, and Henry Mark—thank you for sharing your father's (and your family's) legacy with me. Thanks to Don Wallace, who never worked at AM970 KAKC, but should have. A big thank-you to Sharon King Davis, granddaughter of KAKC's first owner, Sam Avey, for sharing her family history.

Special thanks to Maggie Brown, Sharon Terry, and Michelle Place of the Tulsa Historical Society, whose wonderful exhibit, The Big 97: Tulsa's KAKC Radio, ran from June 2011 through 2012. Your assistance and generosity helped make this project happen. Thanks also to THS intern Becky Leedy. A big thank-you is owed to Rebecca Peak for her assistance with the layout of this book.

I would also like to extend my gratitude to John Wooley, Cathy Leonard Otey, Sonny Hollingshead, Stacy Richardson, Gary Reynolds, Phil Hall, George Kravis, Don King, Mike Miller and Barbara Smith, Clyde Cole III, Lee Hubby, Sharon Watkins Rue, George Leslie Thomas, Nancy Schallner, Rich Linihan, Jill Henry-Riley, and Kathleen Kennedy.

Thank you to Dial-Global, the company that inherited the KAKC Drake-Chenault logo, which is used with their permission.

I am indebted to Wayne McCombs for his various pieces of ephemera and for his guidance in putting together this book. I must also thank Rodney Echohawk, Judith Nole, Michael Dean of the Oklahoma History Center, Larry O'Dell of the Oklahoma Historical Society, and Eric Rothenbueler. Thanks to researchers Connie Krute, Chris Lair, and the research department of the Tulsa City/County Library, and to Andra Lupardus of McFarlin Library, Hilary Pittman of the *Tulsa World*, and to Mike Ransom's website, *Tulsa TV Memories*.

A word of gratitude to my coworkers at Public Radio Tulsa, KWGS 89.5: P. Casey Morgan has been my partner in celebrating KAKC, and Rich Fisher and Frank Christel have, with a boundless tolerance for all things KAKC, helped me realize my dream of preserving this rich part of Tulsa's radio history.

Thank you to my editor, Winnie Rodgers Timmons, for your guidance and patience during this project.

Many books and reference materials contributed to the telling of this story, including the archives of both the *Tulsa World* and the *Tulsa Tribune*, *Broadcasting Yearbook*, and *Radio & Records*.

Introduction

In there we were all in one place, a generation lost in space.

—"American Pie" by Don McLean

For baby boomers raised in the Tulsa area from the mid-1950s to the mid-1970s, the mere mention of the iconic call letters K-A-K-C brings a smile. They are also likely to bring to mind a story—of winning a contest, picking up the weekly record survey, or attending a sock hop or concert. And, of course, listening to KAKC constantly.

KAKC-AM970 was the legendary Top 40 station that dominated radio listening in the Tulsa area like no other station before or since. According to the ratings services of the day, Hooper and Pulse, during its peak in the late 1950s and early 1960s, the station claimed half of all radio listening in the Tulsa area, while the other half-dozen AM stations split the remaining 50 percent. That is an astonishing statistic; these days, when a radio station captures five percent of the audience, it is cause for celebration.

Boomers who grew up in and around Tulsa, whose nickname at the time was "the Magic Empire," might also recall the name of their favorite KAKC deejay, possibly Scooter Segraves, Dick Schmitz, Lee Bayley, Mike McCarthy, or one of the other top-notch talents who sat down at a KAKC microphone. Name recognition for these bona fide rock stars of their day has endured, as Bayley discovered on a mid-2000s Tulsa visit, when the first person he saw, the woman at the rental-car counter, asked him to sign an autograph. It had been 40 years since his last show in the area.

When the New KAKC exploded onto the scene in the latter half of 1956 with its Top 40 (or, at KAKC, Top 50) format, it was something completely different. Up until that time, Tulsa radio stations had been following a network schedule similar to that of a modern-day television station. Each radio station offered a variety of music and talk programs—including dramas, comedies, and variety shows—with the most popular shows coming from a network. Listeners looked up the program they wanted from the radio guide in the newspaper, tuned to the station for that show, then, in theory, tuned out, much like television viewers of today. In other words, their allegiance was to the particular shows they liked, rather than to the radio station itself.

This model worked well in the pre-television era. From radio's beginnings in the 1920s through the Great Depression of the 1930s and World War II in the 1940s, AM radio, with its theater-of-the-mind shows and fireside chats, was the American family's primary source for information and entertainment.

The 1950s and television changed everything. Networks reprioritized, moving classic radio shows (and the revenue they generated for local stations) to television. By the mid-1950s, radio was in crisis. By 1960, everything had changed, from the devices themselves to the sounds they emitted and the ways in which the audience listened to them.

The medium's rebirth was format radio. Bucking the pattern in which trends began on the coasts and spread inward, format radio was born and nurtured in the Midwest.

Around 1950, Todd Storz, the young owner of KOWH, Omaha, Nebraska, began featuring local deejays playing the top recordings from the hit parade, over and over. Storz reasoned that if they played a popular song at 10:00 a.m., they would need to play it again a couple of hours later for a completely different group of listeners. It proved to be a winning strategy. When those deejay shows became more popular than the other programs on the station, they were expanded around the clock; thus, format radio was born.

With format radio, each station had a consistency of sound 24 hours a day instead of a mixed bag of shows. This model is still in place today. Whether a station plays Top 40, country, some other kind of music, or a form of talk programming, the station sounds pretty much the same around the clock. Instead of tuning in for a specific show, listeners select and build a relationship with a station that best fits their tastes and lifestyle.

By 1954, Storz was so successful that he expanded his empire, purchasing WTIX in New Orleans and WHB in Kansas City and installing his new format in both cities. In New Orleans, one of Storz competitors, WDSU, had a show that counted down the Top 20 songs from the hit parade every afternoon. So WTIX started their countdown one hour earlier and extended it one hour later, making it a Top 40 countdown. The term "Top 40" stuck as the name for the format with repeated plays of the top hits.

That same year, radio owner Gordon McClendon, a friend and disciple of Storz, brought Top 40 to his struggling station in Dallas, Texas, KLIF-AM1190. McClendon added exciting contests and games to his Top 40 mix, and KLIF soon dominated the ratings.

Societal and technological changes created a kind of perfect storm for Top 40 radio to succeed. Oklahoma author and music historian John Wooley explains, "by the late 1950s, the first wave of Americans born after World War II were approaching their teenage years, and the 'baby boom generation' as they were later called, were more mobile and had more spending money than previous generations. And they were the perfect audience." By mid-decade, a new style of music, rock and roll, showed up in the Top 40. When the song "Rock Around The Clock" by Bill Haley & His Comets hit No. 1 on the Billboard charts in March 1955, the rock-and-roll era had officially begun.

At the very same time, transistor technology transformed portable radios from bulky lunch-box sized sets to something small enough and light enough to fit into a coat pocket. Transistor radios made listening to the radio a personal experience. "Unless you lived it, it may be hard for you to understand the importance radio played in our lives back then," Wooley says. "When KAKC came along and they were playing our generation's music and the deejays were talking to *us*, it was very special." KAKC began playing Top 40 full time in the latter half of 1956 and shot straight to the top of the ratings.

Using transistor radios, listeners took KAKC with them everywhere they went, even to bed, tucking the transistor under the pillow and listening on the one plastic earpiece. They heard Elvis, the Beatles, teen idols, girl groups, and Motown performers, and then purchased their favorites on 45-rpm records at Bill's "T" Records or at Woolworth's or JC Penney.

In those days, the Top 40 included music by artists like Frank Sinatra and Dean Martin and songs by country music stars like Johnny Cash and Tammy Wynette. There was also always a good dose of instrumental songs—KAKC played it all. The Big 97 is also where local listeners first heard Led Zeppelin, Jimi Hendrix, and Eric Clapton in the big melting pot of the Top 40 playlist.

But to imply that KAKC was so dominant simply because it played Top 40 music would be grossly incorrect. The New KAKC was a cut above on so many levels, including community service. Even the people who could not warm up to the younger generation's music conceded this point. The station was always out doing something positive in the community, whether it was raising money for a specific charity, increasing awareness for better firefighting equipment for Tulsa, or putting on an Easter egg hunt for the entire city. And while KAKC did not invent mobile news, they excelled at it, providing coverage whenever and wherever breaking news happened in the Tulsa area.

The Big 7 deejays, later called the Big 97 jocks, held an elevated status in our lives. Radio blogger Steven Holcombe put it well, saying, "I remember when the DJ was almost at the same level as the musician, at least to the radio listener, and when each radio station had a personality, not just a format. That personality that you encountered every day became a part of your life." Former Big 97 jocks Jim Peters and Robert W. Walker both recall being treated like the Beatles by fans in Tulsa. "Happy" Harry Wilson remembers once being on a podium with then Oklahoma governor J. Howard Edmondson. While several people approached Wilson because he was with KAKC, no one paid any particular attention to Edmondson.

There is an artistry to being a deejay. The good ones—and there were many through the years at KAKC—were like standup comedians who condensed their jokes and observations into 10- to 15-second windows of time, often over the musical introduction of a song. While comedy in general is about timing, deejays faced the added pressure of making up jokes throughout a shift, starting to tell one while a song begins in the background, and timing the punch line to finish a split second before the artist starts singing. And there were no redos in live radio.

There is a consensus among both listeners and his own peers that Scooter Segraves was the very best at this on-the-fly, exact-timing art, not just in Tulsa, but anywhere. "Segraves's mind is wired differently than ours," contends former Big 97 jock Beau Weaver, referencing Segraves's unique brand of humor and use of the English language. From the mind of Segraves came "albino aardvarques" and "earwigs," but somehow, the way he put it together, it all made sense.

KAKC's history can be divided into distinct eras. KAKC was born as "the Hometown Station" in 1946, broadcasting a lot of sporting events from the Coliseum. The "New" KAKC emerged with Top 40 music in 1956, shot to No. 1 in the ratings, and stayed there for an entire decade. After a brief stumble, when rival Top 40 station KELI 1430 beat them in the ratings, the Big 97 roared back to No. 1 under the direction of Bill Drake, the California consultant who revolutionized the way Top 40 stations sounded in the late 1960s. It was Drake's voice listeners heard saying, "and the hits just keep on comin'."

The Rockin' 97 of the 1970s, with deejays Mike "Morning Mouth" McCarthy, Gary "Ono" Stevens, Charlie Derek, and Scooter Segraves, kept Tulsans listening to AM radio until FM stations like KMOD 97.5, KRAV 96.5, KWEN-FM 95.5 and KTFX 103.3 drew music listeners away from AM for good.

KAKC moved from contemporary to legend at 12:00 noon on January 1, 1979, when, after 22 years as a Top 40 station, it changed to an easy-listening format. The station was sold to a religious broadcaster one year later.

Growing up with the "Drake" KAKC, I was profoundly influenced by what I heard. At 13, I knew what I wanted to be: a radio deejay. Years later, in the 1980s, I had the pleasure of working with one of my idols, Scooter Segraves, at a well-programmed but little-remembered Tulsa station called Magic 99.

Through my friendships with Segraves and Dick Schmitz, I began documenting KAKC's rich history. When I became operations director at Public Radio 89.5 in Tulsa (an NPR affiliate), my boss, Rich Fisher, suggested that I could do a radio documentary. I admit that part of my attraction to the project was purely selfish. I wanted to spend time with these people again, to hear their voices and listen to their stories. I wanted to know what it was like to work at KAKC, and I was curious about how they viewed their time there all these years later.

The result was the radio documentary *Tulsa's Top 40 Legend, KAKC, The Big 97*, which aired in two hour-long installments on KWGS 89.5 in September 2010. It won the Oklahoma Association of Broadcasters Best Special Programming award in 2011 and received a finalist award at the New York Festivals, an international competition. You can order it at www.kakcradio.com

That project led to KWGS 89.5's partnership with the Tulsa Historical Society on the exhibit, The Big 97: Tulsa's KAKC Radio. The well-received installation, designed by THS's Maggie Brown, ran from June 2011 to October 2012. At its opening reception, a standing-room-only crowd listened intently as Scooter Segraves; Dick Schmitz; Harry Wilson; Clayton Vaughn; Mike McCarthy; Steve Suttle; and Mary Alice (Mark) Alexander, daughter of KAKC owner S. Carl Mark, took turns recounting what it was like to work at the top radio station of its era.

The legendary air staff came back in July 2012 for a second party at the THS, billed as a "sock hop with the KAKC deejays."

Many of the images from the THS exhibit appear in this book. Additionally, numerous quotes that accompany these photographs are from the KWGS documentary.

I have often thought that it is too bad there exists no archive of local radio shows from the Top 40 era. It is too bad that you can't listen to a Scooter Segraves show from 1967 as easily as you can call up an old *Bewitched* TV episode. But such was the nature of live, local radio: those broadcasts were of their time. That funny thing the deejay said while playing your favorite song perfectly captured that moment before disappearing into thin air.

But we still have our memories. And now, we have some images to go along with them, along with commentary from some of the people who entertained us during those carefree days of youth.

South Peoria between Thirty-first Street and Fifty-first Street is a Tulsa neighborhood called Brookside. But to baby boomers it was also known as "the restless ribbon," where high school students from Tulsa and surrounding communities came to cruise. The ribbon's one mandatory stop was Pennington's Drive-Inn restaurant. Pictured in 1956 shortly after it opened, Pennington's was known for delicacies like jumbo fried shrimp and black-bottom pie. On the weekends and during those endless summer nights when a steady stream of cars cruised Pennington's, it was possible to hear a continuous wall of KAKC sound. (Courtesy of Beryl Ford/Rotary Club of Tulsa Collection of the Tulsa City-County Library and Tulsa Historical Society.)

One

The Hometown Station

KAKC began not as a Top 40 or rock-and-roll station, but as "the Hometown Station." When Tulsa's fifth commercial radio station came on the air, it was at 1570 on the dial.

The Coliseum was an ornate indoor arena in downtown Tulsa that took up a city block between Fifth and Sixth Streets on Elgin Avenue. The massive 4,500-seat venue held all manner of events, from conventions and graduations to rodeos, hockey games, and wrestling competitions. Tulsa civic leader Sam Avey purchased the building in 1944. As owner of the Tulsa Ice Oilers hockey team and a promoter of professional wrestling, Avey saw the advantage of having a radio station. In 1946, with business partners R.W. Kellough and veteran Tulsa broadcaster Glenn Condon, he received the license for a daytime-only radio station with the call letters K-A-K-C. The first *K* was assigned by the Federal Communications Commission, and the other letters stood for the owners: *A* for Avey, *K* for Kellough, and *C* for Condon.

On Christmas Eve 1946, the station signed on with a two-hour broadcast of the Christmas party for children, an annual Coliseum event hosted by Avey and his daughter Pat. With studios in the popular venue's basement, the early KAKC broadcast local news, music shows, hockey, wrestling, and other sporting events held in the building. The station also carried Tulsa Oilers baseball, with KAKC sports director Mack Creager handling the play-by-play.

Additionally, Avey was granted a license to broadcast on the newly created FM broadcast band, touted for its static-free reception. Beginning in 1947, sporting events from the Coliseum were broadcast on both KAKC-AM1570 and KAKC-FM95.5; however, because there were so few FM radios in the marketplace, the FM broadcasts were discontinued after a couple of years.

During this era, KAKC-AM moved to its well-known 970 dial position. On the evening of September 20, 1952, lightning sparked a spectacular fire that burned the Coliseum to the ground. The building had been empty at the time except for two KAKC employees, who managed to escape unharmed. The station broadcast from their transmitter site near the corner of Twenty-first Street and Yale Avenue until new studios were secured in the American Airlines building at 910 South Boston.

When it opened in 1929, the Coliseum was called the "Showplace of the Southwest" and Tulsa's new "Palace of Wonders." The brick-and-terracotta structure, with a price tag of nearly $1 million, opened on New Year's Day, 1929, with the Tulsa Ice Oilers' very first hockey game. The facility became a vital gathering place for the city of Tulsa. KAKC's first studios were in the northeast corner of the basement. (Courtesy of Sharon King Davis.)

Announcer Frank Morrow is pictured at the control board of the KAKC studios in 1951. Morrow recalls running the console for radio preachers and engineering re-creations of out-of-town Tulsa Oilers baseball games. Sports director Mack Creager did the play-by-play from the bare-bones description of the game from the wire service. Thanks to Creager's imagination and Morrow's recorded sound effects, those in-studio broadcasts sounded like they were live from the ball game. (Courtesy of Frank Morrow.)

Sam Avey, KAKC's first owner, had a colorful life. Born in Kingfisher, Oklahoma, in 1895, Avey spent his young adulthood traveling the vaudeville circuit as an actor and prop man. After a stint in the grocery business in Cherryvale, Kansas, he moved to Tulsa in 1924 and became involved in sports management, promoting boxing and professional wrestling. He later started Tulsa's first pro-football team and the Tulsa Oilers ice hockey team. In 1942, Avey purchased the Coliseum. He founded KAKC-AM and KAKC-FM four years later. Avey was well known for his support of children's charities, including the Babies Milk Fund, for which he held a benefit wrestling event each year. For many years, Avey hosted an annual Christmas party for Tulsa's children, and he also chaired the Oklahoma Santa Claus Commission, providing Christmas gifts for orphans across the state. He served as president of both the Downtown Rotary Club and the chamber of commerce and was one of the founders of Tulsa's F&M Bank. Avey was posthumously inducted into the Tulsa Hall of Fame in 2006. (Courtesy of Sharon King Davis.)

Ramon L. King hosted a daytime show on KAKC in the early 1950s. King (right, in this photograph) is in the studio with an unidentified guest. King was married to Sam Avey's daughter Pat and is the father of Tulsa developer and civic leader Sharon King Davis. Davis says she has many fond memories of KAKC as a little girl, listening to her dad and hearing about everything that was going on around town. (Courtesy of Sharon King Davis.)

The early KAKC was big on sports. They broadcast local events from the Coliseum and carried national sports franchises through the Liberty Broadcasting System and, later, Mutual Radio. KAKC sports director Mack Creager hosted two sports shows a day and did play-by-play for Tulsa Oilers baseball. Creager made a successful segue to television, becoming a well-liked sportscaster for KOTV Channel 6, the CBS affiliate, in the 1960s. (Courtesy of Nancy Schallner.)

Glenn Condon, the C in KAKC, was already a 35-year veteran of newspaper and radio in Tulsa when he joined Sam Avey in founding the station. Condon handled the on-air news reports. In a long journalistic career that began shortly after statehood, Condon had literally seen it all as an eyewitness to Tulsa's transition from small town to the "Oil Capital of the World." He finished out his career on KRMG AM740. (Courtesy of Beryl Ford/ Rotary Club of Tulsa Collection of the Tulsa City-County Library and Tulsa Historical Society.)

On December 24, 1950, KAKC owners Sam Avey (left) and R.W. Kellough (center) joined Avey's granddaughter Sharon King in celebrating the start of KAKC's fifth year of broadcasting. Avey used the occasion to announce the addition of the Liberty Broadcasting System, hence the "KAKC LBS" written on the cake. Liberty's daily broadcasts from the United Nations and major league baseball games supplemented the station's local sports programs. (Courtesy of Sharon King Davis.)

Tulsa firefighters battle the Coliseum fire on September 20, 1952. Eyewitnesses reported seeing a bright flash of lightning before the building was ignited. The massive structure's wooden ceiling accelerated the blaze. The contents of the building, including KAKC'S studios, were a total loss. KOTV Channel 6, with studios just down the street on Elgin Avenue, rolled a TV camera onto their roof and broadcast the spectacular blaze to their audience. It was the first live-on-the-scene broadcast in Tulsa television history. (Courtesy of Tulsa Historical Society.)

KAKC's next home was in the American Airlines building at 910 South Boston Avenue, featured in this c. 1950 photograph. From KAKC's 12th-floor studios on the south side of the building, station personnel had a view of the Arkansas River. This came in handy when reporting on the devastating floods of the late 1950s. (Courtesy of Beryl Ford/Rotary Club of Tulsa Collection of the Tulsa City-County Library and Tulsa Historical Society.)

Two

THE "NEW" KAKC

In 1955, KAKC was sold to the Rev. Forrest G. Conley, pastor of Tulsa's Revival Tabernacle Church on Second Street and Elwood Avenue. However, Conley's ownership of the station is a mere footnote; after a year of featuring Conley's sermons and programs from the Mutual Broadcasting System, KAKC was sold to Houston advertising executive Lester Kamin.

Meanwhile, there was a big shift occurring in popular music. A new style called rock and roll was showing up in movies and on TV. When the song "Rock Around The Clock" by Bill Haley & His Comets hit No. 1 on the Billboard charts in 1955, the rock-and-roll era had officially begun. The new music, characterized by electric guitars and a heavy beat, was finding its way into Tulsa clubs and into the city's premier record shop, Bill's "T" Records. KTUL-AM1430 announcer Don Wallace noticed that rockabilly records were selling at Bill's "T" Records, so he began playing them on his four daily radio shows on KTUL that were sandwiched in between CBS network programs such as *Arthur Godfrey Time*, *The Guiding Light*, and *Gunsmoke*. Wallace recalls getting great ratings when he began playing rock and rockabilly by Elvis Presley and Carl Perkins. Wallace had a fan club, played the first teen hops in Tulsa, and championed Elvis's first Tulsa concert on April 18, 1956, at the Fairgrounds Pavilion. He was even mentioned on national television during a Presley appearance on the Steve Allen Show for his petition, signed by hundreds of Tulsa fans, to bring Elvis back for another concert.

Weeknights at 10:00 p.m., KTUL had Frank Berry's *Rhythm Roundup*. African American deejay Berry amassed quite a following playing what was sometimes referred to as "sex music," featuring artists like Hank Ballard and the Midnighters and LeVern Baker. Berry purchased his time from the station and sold his own commercials. But KTUL management did not want to play rock and roll full-time.

When KAKC came on with Top 40 radio 24 hours a day in the latter half of 1956, they shot to the top of the local ratings and stayed there for an entire decade.

RADIO STATION LOG—Thursday, Dec. 2, 1954

TIME	CBS KTUL 1430	KOME 1300	NBC KVOO 1170	MBS KAKC 970	ABC KRMG 740
5:30		Hr of Inspiration	Family Worship	Coffee Cup Caprs	Earl Bird Show
5:45		"	Science Serv Ag	"	"
6:00	Morning Ramble	News	Today's 1st Hdl	Coffee Cup Caprs	News-Weath Mkt
6:15	"	Hymns You Love	Rural News	"	Early Bird Show
6:30	"	Family Devotion	News of Hour	"	Akin Special
6:45	Vic Lndbrg News	" :55 News	Rural Rt. 1170	"	"
7:00	CBS World News	Charlie & Earl	Alex Dreier	Coffee Cup	News
7:15	Morning Watch	Blackwood Bros.	Wiley & Gene	Capers	Music on the
7:30	"	Gleaner Brdcast	Singing Clock	Bradley News	Sunny Side
7:45	" :55—Sports	United Drys	News of the Hour	Coffee Cup	Don Hughes
8:00	News from Home	Full Gospel Hour	Eggs at Eight	Capers with	Breakfast Club
8:15	Morning Watch	"	"	John Trotter	"
8:30	Roy Pickett show	Word of God	"	Youth Evangelist	"
8:45	:55—News	"	Lady of the	"	"
9:00	Arthur Godfrey	Glorious Gospel	Bob Smith Show	Old Time	My True Story
9:15	"	Music & Musings	"	Religion	"
9:30	"	John Brown Hour	"	Voice of Healing	Wspering Streets
9:45	"	"	Break The Bank	"	When Girl Mar.
10:00	Arthur Godfrey	Steve Pringle	Strike It Rich	Florida Calling	Modrn Romances
10:15	"	"	"	"	Kitchen Club
10:30	Make Up Mind	Mid Morning	Phrase that Pays	Queen for a Day	News
10:45	You Win	Masterworks	Second Chance	"	Brunch Time
11:00	Windy Warren	News—: 5	Ma Perkins	Break the Bank	Brunch Time
11:15	Aunt Jenny	For Ladies Only	Tulsa Talks	Vocal Time	"
11:30	Helen Trent	"	Back to The	Meet Mary Lou	"
11:45	Our Gal Sunday	Noon News	Bible	"	Glenn Condon
12:00	Vic Lundberg	Luncheon	News of Hour	Cedric Foster	Best in the West
12:15	Lewis Meyer	Serenade	Johnny Lee Wills	News Deadline	"
12:30	Young Dr Mlone	"	"	Ted Steele Show	Leon McAuliffe
12:45	Guiding Light	"	Farm Profit	"	Best in the West
1:00	2nd Mrs. Burton	Peter Slack Time	Sons of Range	Story Time with	Dr. E.F. Webber
1:15	Road of Life	"	"	Madeleine	"
1:30	Nora Drake	Mid Day Magic	Music Market	Wonderful City	Sheila Graham
1:45	Brighter Day	"	Judy and Jane	"	Bandstand
2:00	Hilltop House	News :05 Mid	News	Moore's Melody	Tulsa Ballroom
2:15	Houseparty	Day Magic	Woman in Love	Shop with Jack	with Joe Knight
2:30	"	Music You Want	Pepper Young	Moore	"
2:45	Automobile show	When You	Rght to Happinss	"	"
3:00	Roy Pickett show	Want It	Backstage Wife	Melody Shop	Condon. News
3:15	"	"	Stella Dallas	Tony Martin	Tulsa Ballroom
3:30	"	Waltz Time	Young Widder	"T" Record	"
3:45	"	"	Wom in my Hse	AQ Chickn News	"
4:00	Vic Lundberg	News—:05	Just Plain Bill	"T" Record	News
4:15	Frank Morrow	Music Room	Lorenzo Jones	Presents	Tulsa Ballroom
4:30	Show	Piano Reveries	Hotel for Pets	Lewis Meyer	"
4:45	Silver $ Man	"	Pays to Be Mar	"	"
5:00	Vic Lundberg	News :05 Side-	News Briefs	Sergeant Preston	News :05 Weathr
5:15	Land We Love	walk Cafe	Perry Mason	of the Yukon	Tulsa Ballroom
5:30	The Best By	Voices in the Air	Sagebrush Sere.	Sentimental	:40 Sport Lights:
5:45	News Roundup	Sports Review	News of Hour	Journey	Bill Stern
6:00	Tennessee Ernie	Evening News	Spotlight Review	Fulton Lewis Jr.	Glenn Condon
6:15	Lowell Thomas	Singspiration	Spotlight Review	News Deadline	Three Suns
6:30	Film Fare	John Brown Hour	Morgan Beatty	Gabriel Heatter	Silver Eagle
6:45	Edw. R. Murrow	"	One Man's Fam.	Meet the Artist	" :55 News
7:00	Suspense	News :05 Minia-	Roy Rogers	Official Detective	Guy Lombardo
7:15	" :25 News	ture Concert	Family	"	Vandercook
7:30	Night Watch	Family Favorites	Bob Hope Show	Crime Fighters	Western Rndup
7:45	"	"	"	"	"
8:00	Rsemry Clooney	Concert	Spend a Million	Bill Henry	Serenade Room
8:15	Bing Crosby	Hall of the Air	"	Mutual Newsreel	"
8:30	Amos 'n' Andy	"	Senior Ben	Cloud Club with	Ralph Flanagan
8:45	" :55—News	"	"	Ron Greene	Show

During the 1950s, the daily radio schedule was printed in the newspaper and in guides such as this *Television and Radio News* magazine for the week of November 28 to December 4, 1954. All five Tulsa commercial radio stations are listed, along with their network affiliations. It resembles the TV schedule of today. Each station offers a variety of shows, from news, to live and recorded music, comedy, drama, sports, and religion. Many of the programs of this era were only 15 minutes in duration. Note that local musicians Leon McAuliffe and Johnny Lee Wills each have radio shows. Tulsa bookseller Lewis Meyer, who would become a staple on Tulsa television for 40 years, manages to have shows on both KTUL and KAKC. Top network shows, like *Arthur Godfrey*, *Perry Mason*, *Guiding Light*, and *Queen for a Day*, would soon make the transition to television, forcing radio to find a new type of programming to remain competitive. In 1956, KAKC would lead that charge with their Top 40 format, introducing Northeastern Oklahoma to the future of radio, where every station has a consistency of sound 24 hours a day. (Courtesy of Wayne McCombs.)

The transistor radio, introduced in the mid-1950s, was a key ingredient in the success of Top 40 radio. Unlike the bulky tube portables that came before, transistor technology made radios small enough, lightweight enough, and affordable enough for boomers to take their favorite radio station everywhere—even to bed, listening on the plastic earpiece that came with the set. This Silvertone model (right) sold at Sears for under $20. (Courtesy of the author.)

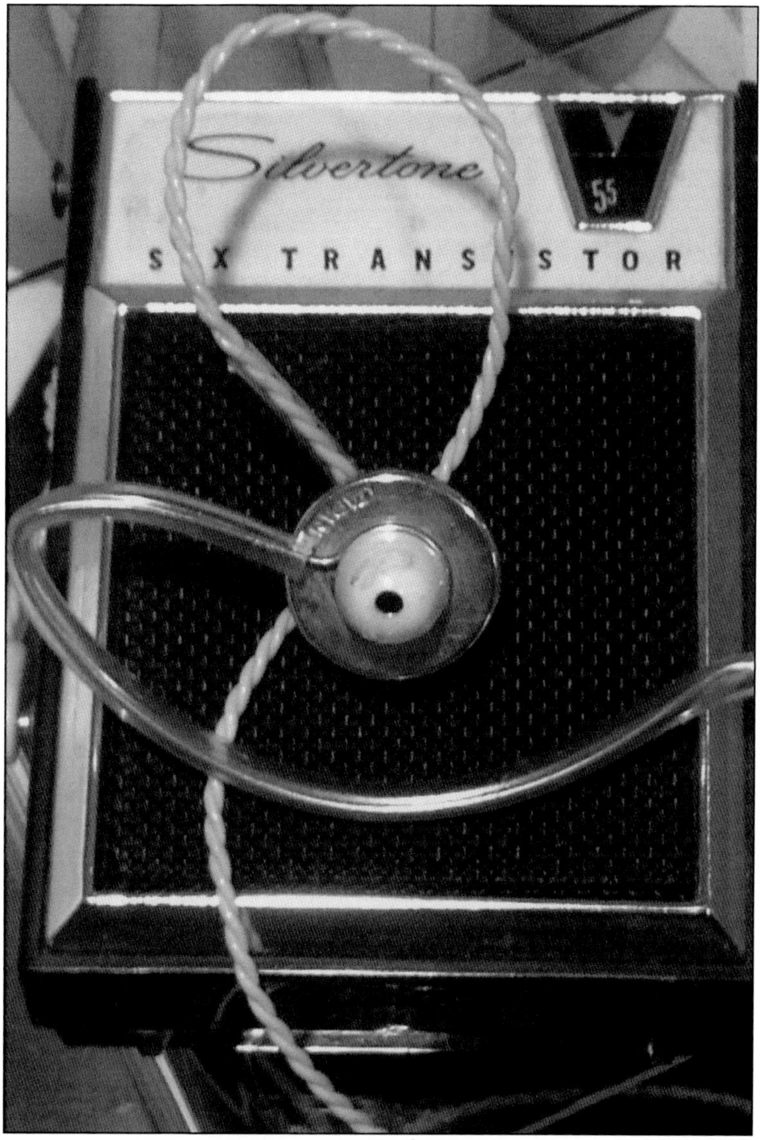

THE NEW KAKC 970

This is the logo most identified with the New KAKC. (Courtesy of the author.)

KAKC had been Tulsa's top station for a few short months when Dick Schmitz joined the station as a mobile newsman in spring 1957. Left, Schmitz poses with his news cruiser that same year in the 800 block of South College Avenue, a neighborhood that is now part of the University of Tulsa campus. Below, Schmitz is seen conducting a mobile news interview at the airport. By late 1958, he was hosting the KAKC morning show and was also promoted to program director. In that role, Schmitz was the principal architect of the station's on-air and promotional efforts for the next eight years. (Both, courtesy of Dick and Alma Schmitz.)

From the beginning, the new KAKC was community-service oriented. "Everything we did had a tie to charity," recalls Dick Schmitz. In this 1959 game of donkey softball, Schmitz mugs for the camera moments before taking a spill and suffering a slight concussion. The doctor who treated him that day became his physician for the next 40 years. (Courtesy of Dick Schmitz.)

KAKC was known for exciting and often unusual promotions, from donkey softball to wheelchair races to broadcasting underwater. They would do almost any stunt for charity. In this KAKC Skate-a-thon, Big 7 deejay skaters Tom York (left) and Harry Wilson (right) pose with referee Don Bromley (center), the manager of the Continental Skating Rink. In the photograph, the skaters are passing the "torch." (Courtesy of Dick Schmitz.)

For the Tulsa Boat Show in January 1959, the Big 7 deejays broadcast their shows underwater. National Tank constructed a special tank, which was then filled with water, and the deejays wore wetsuits and scuba gear outfitted with a special waterproof microphone inside the mask. According to Schmitz, at one point, the window where people could look in developed a crack, which they feared would eventually cause the tank to leak (it did not). (Courtesy of Dick Schmitz.)

Alma and Dick Schmitz pose with singer Connie Francis, right, at a national deejay convention in Miami Beach, Florida. (Courtesy of Dick Schmitz.)

Dick Schmitz (with script in hand, seated at the KAKC microphone) reads a commercial for Quaker State Refining Company. Looking on are Dick Wilhour (left), Pennant Petroleum Company owner and distributor of Quaker State products, and George Harms Jr. (right), representative from Quaker State. (Photograph by Sherman Willsey, courtesy of Dick Schmitz.)

Big 7 deejay Don Kelly simply went by "Kelly" on the air. He had a sidekick, Chauncey, who was largely heard but not seen. Here, Kelly is pictured being pulled by a trained ostrich as part of the entertainment at the Tulsa Horse Show, around 1960. (Courtesy of Dick Schmitz.)

The New KAKC sponsored lots of teen dances (or hops). Many, like this one at the Continental Skating Rink, featured nationally known recording artists. Around 1960, the Diamonds (with their hits "Little Darlin' " and "The Stroll") starred on a bill with Rodney & the Blazers and Merlene Garner. Four of the Big 7 deejays join the artists on stage. Distinguished by their matching plaid jackets, they are, from left to right, Dick Schmitz, Don Kelly, Harry Wilson and Will Jones. (Courtesy of Dick Schmitz.)

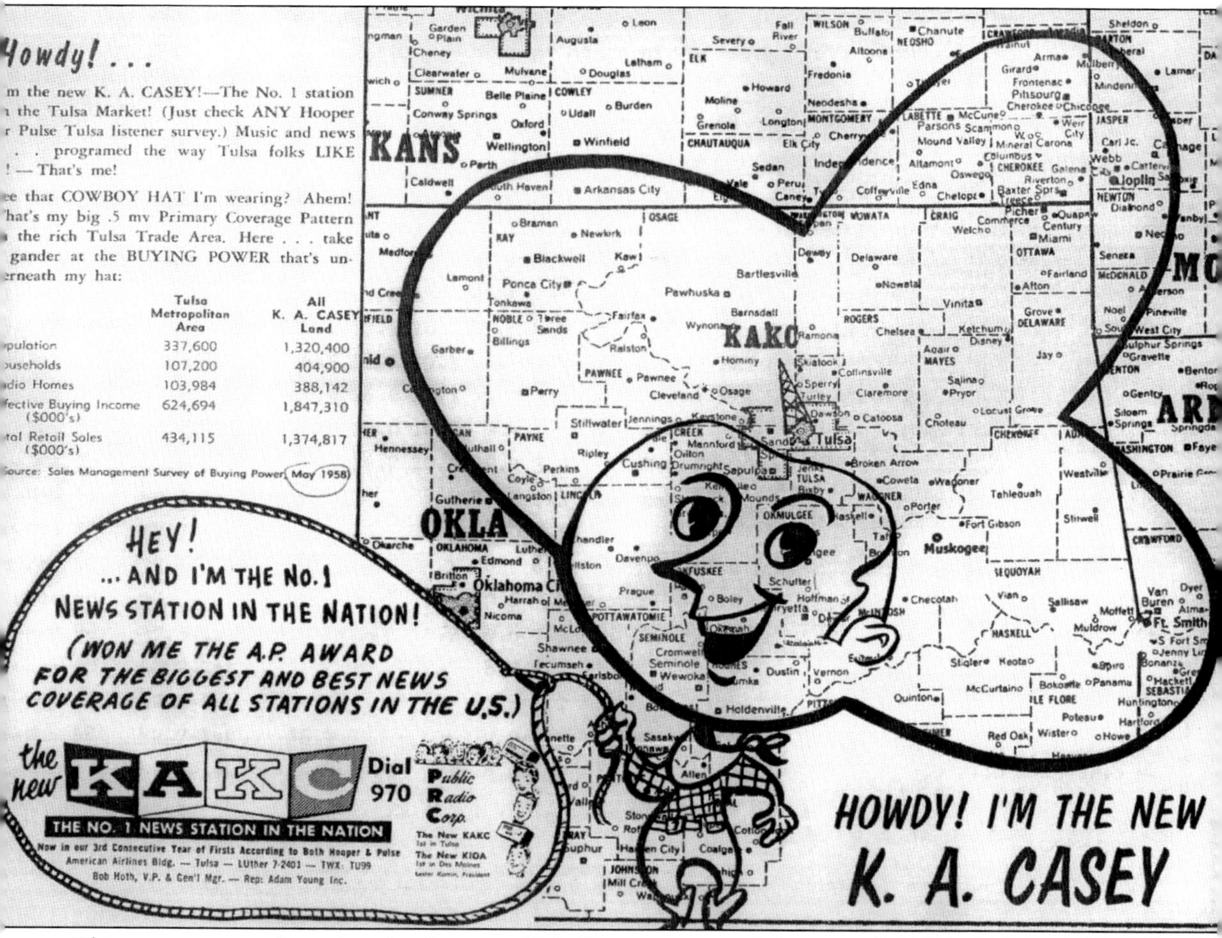

This coverage map featuring the character K.A. Casey was part of the station's 1959 sales materials. Casey touts their No. 1 ratings and news awards from the Associated Press, and his cowboy hat displays the daytime reach of 1000-watt KAKC in northeast Oklahoma and parts of Kansas, Missouri, and Arkansas. What Casey is keeping under his hat is the fact that the station's coverage area was much smaller than those of many of their competitors, especially KVOO AM1170 and KRMG AM740, which blanketed the whole region with 50,000 watts of power. Yet, with regard to listeners in the Tulsa metropolitan area, KAKC dominated. After sunset, when AM970 reduced power further to 500 watts, it was difficult to hear the station clearly in parts of Tulsa and its suburbs—a fact that makes KAKC's stranglehold on the market even more remarkable. "We were smaller in terms of power and coverage," acknowledges Dick Schmitz, "but no one knew that. What the Big 7 deejays did was to try to make everything they did sound so exciting that people would do whatever they had to in order to listen." (Courtesy of John Durkee.)

Harry Wilson began his career at KWGS at the University of Tulsa and worked at KTUL 1430 before joining KAKC in 1958. In his eight years there, Wilson worked as a Big 7 deejay; mobile newsman; and, during his last three years, news director. Pictured at the news desk (above) and with his mobile news unit (below) Wilson was one of the principal contributors to KAKC's halcyon years. (Both, courtesy of Harry Wilson.)

Many stars of the day stopped by the KAKC studios when they were in town. Annette Funicello, one of the original Mouseketeers of Walt Disney's *The Mickey Mouse Club*, came to Tulsa on a promotional tour and dropped by to chat with Big 7 deejay Harry Wilson. Below, Wilson interviews singer/songwriter/teen idol Paul Anka (left). (Both, courtesy of Harry Wilson.)

The Annual Easter Egg Hunt, one of KAKC's early signature events, drew thousands of people to Mohawk Park and other locations around Tulsa each spring. The KAKC newsletter of April 1964 says of that year's event, "it took many hours for the KAKC bunny rabbit to stuff 36,000 eggs with gift certificates good for prizes and many more hours to "lay" them at the three hunt areas in Tulsa. But it took only 90 seconds for the thousands of Tulsa boys and girls to completely scour the area and retrieve every one of the gaily-colored plastic eggs." KAKC eventually discontinued the event simply because the crowds had become too large. (Both, courtesy of Dick Schmitz.)

In the early days, the Big 7 deejays wore matching jackets with red sewn-on patches that identified them as members of this prestigious group. Note that Dick Schmitz, below, is wearing his as he hands out giveaway albums to the crowd at a late 1950s KAKC Easter Egg Hunt. (Both, courtesy of Dick Schmitz.)

The New KAKC was a threat on so many levels. In addition to the appeal of its Top 40 music, the news department became known for on-the-spot reporting and excellence in general, winning numerous awards through the years. Here, members of the KAKC news staff pose with other 1957 award winners in the Tulsa market. Pictured are, from left to right, Ed Montray of KRMG, Bud Curry and Dick Schmitz of KAKC, Glenn Condon of KRMG, and an unidentified KCCO employee. Condon, of course, had been one of KAKC's original owners in the 1940s and is the C in KAKC. (Courtesy of Dick Schmitz.)

Record labels often give awards, such as gold records, to radio stations in recognition of the station's role in giving their artists and songs exposure. Big 7 deejays Harry Wilson, Chris Lane and Dick Schmitz receive a record company award. The Doris Day and Duke Ellington albums in the background are releases of the company giving the recognition. (Courtesy of Dick Schmitz.)

Harry Wilson poses for a feature article in the national magazine *TV-Radio-Mirror*. The 1960 article about Wilson's top-rated KAKC morning show mentioned "Happy" Harry's cheerful, optimist approach to his work and also pictured him at home with his wife, Doris, and two young daughters. (Courtesy of Harry Wilson.)

The immensely popular Kingston Trio was in Tulsa for a sold-out concert in 1959 and, as many groups did in those days, came to KAKC for a visit to promote their performance. Pictured from left to right are Dave Guard, Bob Shane, Big 7 deejay Harry Wilson, and Nick Reynolds. (Courtesy of Harry Wilson.)

In the late 1950s, KAKC began promoting local beauty pageants. This Miss KAKC, Anita Bryant, became Miss Tulsa, then Miss Oklahoma, and ultimately represented the state in the Miss America pageant in Atlantic City, where she finished a respectable second runner-up. Bryant, pictured in her swimsuit during the Miss Tulsa pageant, became a nationally known recording artist ("Paper Roses" reached No. 5 in Billboard) and a spokesperson for Florida orange juice. Bryant gained even more fame in the 1970s and 1980s as an outspoken opponent of the gay lifestyle. (Courtesy of Dick Schmitz.)

In order to promote Miss KAKC Anita Bryant's participation in the 1958 Miss America pageant in Atlantic City, the station created a special promotional flier. Artist Richard (Richut) Ruhl, who had been an animator for Disney, portrays Bryant as Snow White, while the Big 7 deejays are assigned with the characteristics of the seven dwarfs. Because he did the morning show, Dick Schmitz was "Sleepy." Also featured are "Happy" Harry Wilson and "Bashful" Kelly. This promotional flier was handed out to hundreds of motorists at a Turner Turnpike rest stop by the Tulsa Jaycees. (Courtesy of Dick Schmitz.)

Anita Bryant (left) is pictured at a public appearance in costume as Chauncey, a character on Don Kelly's KAKC radio show. Beside her is Dick Schmitz. (Courtesy of Dick Schmitz.)

Mary Ann Hazelton (left), Miss KAKC 1959, poses with her 1960 successor, Mary Ann Bell. Both women went on to become Miss Tulsa, and Hazelton went on to win the Miss Oklahoma pageant. (Courtesy of Dick Schmitz.)

Big 7 deejays Bob Brown and Dick Schmitz visit with two of the contestants in the KAKC-sponsored Miss Teenage Tulsa pageant at Tulsa Book & Record Shop. Pictured are, from left to right, Bob Brown, Diane Bennett, Leanne Turner, and Dick Schmitz. (Courtesy of Dick Schmitz.)

Miss Tulsa 1959, Mary Ann Hazelton, is pictured in the KAKC control room with Dick Schmitz, (seated) who is holding Hazelton's crown. (Courtesy of Dick Schmitz.)

KAKC was the station to hear Elvis Presley music in the Tulsa area. Presley first performed in Tulsa in 1956 at the Fairgrounds Pavilion and returned several times through the years in concert at the Civic Assembly Center. This Elvis Christmas card to KAKC is from the mid-1960s. Little Anthony and the Imperials were a rhythm and blues vocal group known for lead singer Jerome "Little Anthony" Gourdine's falsetto vocals on soulful ballads such as "Goin' out of My Head," "Hurt So Bad," and "Tears on My Pillow." KAKC received this Christmas card from the band in 1965. (Both, courtesy of Dick Schmitz.)

While working in KAKC mobile news, Harry Wilson endeared himself to the Tulsa Fire Department. Wilson was known for his early arrival on the scene to report fires and also for promoting the efforts and needs of local firefighters. In appreciation, Chief J.C. "Jelly" Sanders presented Wilson with a complete firefighter's bunker outfit: helmet, boots, and all. Sanders told him they gave him the suit so he would not burn his clothes at three-alarm fires. Above, Wilson hams it up with Chief Sanders. Below, KAKC news director Clayton Vaughn instructs Wilson on the proper use of his equipment. (Both, courtesy of Harry Wilson.)

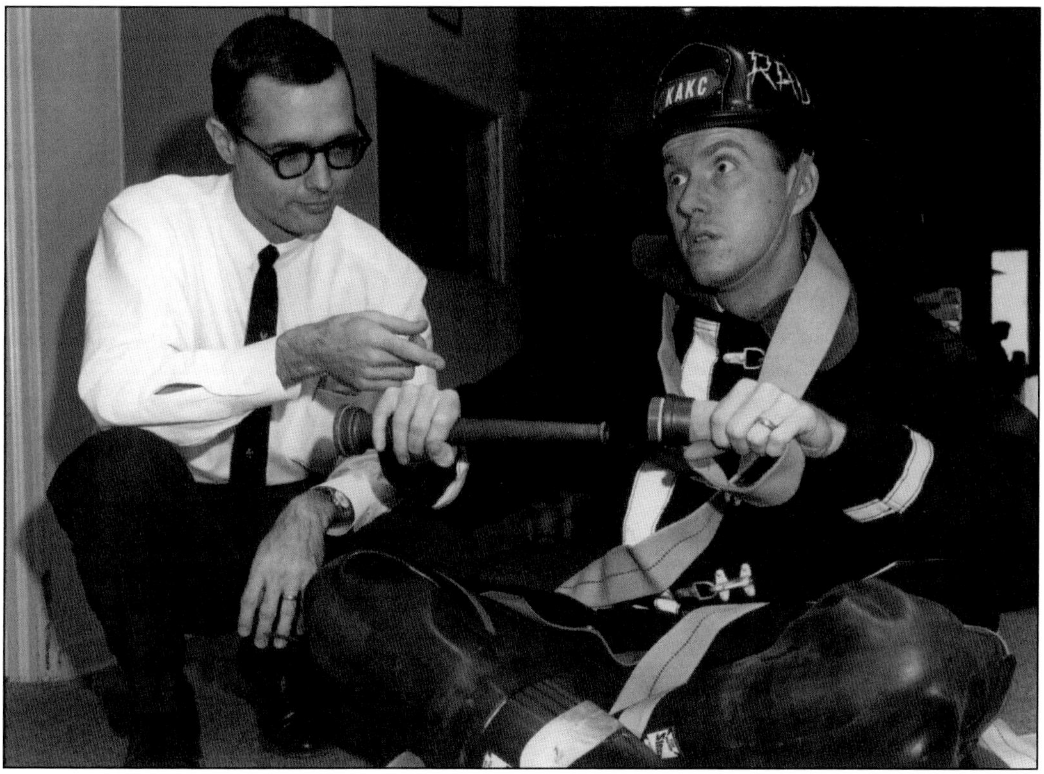

Before Clayton Vaughn became the "Dean of Tulsa Television," he was the news director of KAKC. Under Vaughn's leadership, from 1958 to 1964, AM970 won more Associated Press news awards than any other Tulsa station. Vaughn (center) is pictured inspecting the sign that adorns the airborne addition to the KAKC news arsenal. (Courtesy of Dick Schmitz.)

For several years, Big 7 deejay Harry Wilson was the public address announcer for the Tulsa Oilers, a St. Louis Cardinals farm club. In connection with that, Cardinals manager Bobby Bragen brought close friend and actor Jeff Chandler to KAKC to promote a new movie. Pictured from left to right are Jeff Chandler, Harry Wilson, and Bobby Bragen. (Courtesy of Harry Wilson.)

Harry Wilson and other Big 7 deejays lead a parade of Miss Tulsa State Fair contestants to the fair in the early 1960s. In the foreground, Harry Wilson drives an unidentified contestant. Don Kelly is the driver of the second car. (Courtesy of Dick Schmitz.)

In 1959, a University of Tulsa student named George Basil Segraves III began working at KAKC on the all-night shift. For the radio, the Stuttgart, Arkansas, native used the nickname given to him by his family when he was a small boy: "Scooter." However, working all night and attending TU during the day caused his grades to suffer, so Segraves told his boss, Dick Schmitz, that he was going to have to quit the job he loved. Schmitz offered to switch Segraves to an earlier shift in the evening, and Segraves was able to stay. Thus began a love affair between the deejay and the Tulsa radio audience that would last 17 years. (Courtesy of Dick Schmitz.)

During most of its history as a Top 40 station, KAKC had a station basketball team that played area organizations for charity. The games often benefitted the school or group they were playing. Above, photographed around 1960, the KAKC players perform some on-court antics. Harry Wilson (bottom left corner) ties the official's shoelaces together as Tom York (middle, on the floor) does the same to a member of the opposing team. Dick Schmitz, hand raised in the air, looks on. Below, the KAKC team poses with an unidentified opponent in 1960. The station team members are, from left to right, (first row) Tom Longman, Jerry Adams, Dick Schmitz, Carl Smith, and Will Jones; (second row) Scooter Segraves (holding basketball). (Courtesy of Dick Schmitz.)

As KAKC began its fifth year of first-place ratings in Tulsa, they celebrated with a special edition of the weekly Top 50 record survey. Inside this 8.5-by-11-inch super-sized edition of the survey, listeners could select their favorite songs from the New KAKC's first five years and enter a contest. (Courtesy of Dick Schmitz.)

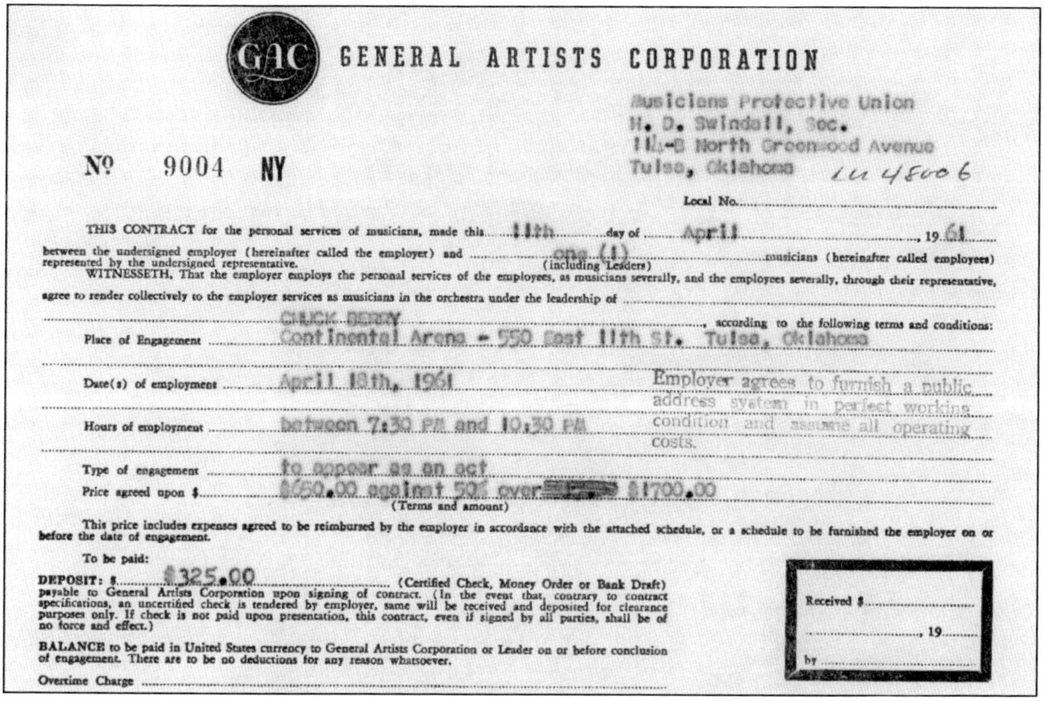

GENERAL ARTISTS CORPORATION

Musicians Protective Union
H. D. Swindall, Sec.
11½-B North Greenwood Avenue
Tulsa, Oklahoma Lu 48006

Nº 9004 NY

Local No. ....

THIS CONTRACT for the personal services of musicians, made this 11th day of April, 1961 between the undersigned employer (hereinafter called the employer) and one (1) (including Leaders) musicians (hereinafter called employees) represented by the undersigned representative.

WITNESSETH, That the employer employs the personal services of the employees, as musicians severally, and the employees severally, through their representative, agree to render collectively to the employer services as musicians in the orchestra under the leadership of CHUCK BERRY, according to the following terms and conditions:

Place of Engagement: Continental Arena - 550 East 11th St. Tulsa, Oklahoma

Date(s) of employment: April 18th, 1961

Hours of employment: between 7:30 PM and 10:30 PM

Employer agrees to furnish a public address system in perfect working condition and assume all operating costs.

Type of engagement: to appear as an act

Price agreed upon $: $650.00 against 50% over [illegible] $1700.00 (Terms and amount)

This price includes expenses agreed to be reimbursed by the employer in accordance with the attached schedule, or a schedule to be furnished the employer on or before the date of engagement.

To be paid:

DEPOSIT: $ $325.00 (Certified Check, Money Order or Bank Draft) payable to General Artists Corporation upon signing of contract. (In the event that, contrary to contract specifications, an uncertified check is tendered by employer, same will be received and deposited for clearance purposes only. If check is not paid upon presentation, this contract, even if signed by all parties, shall be of no force and effect.)

BALANCE to be paid in United States currency to General Artists Corporation or Leader on or before conclusion of engagement. There are to be no deductions for any reason whatsoever.

Overtime Charge ....

Received $ ....
.........., 19 ....
by ....

Several pop music hit makers played KAKC teen hops. Among them was Chuck Berry. As this contract shows, Berry performed at the Continental Skating Rink on April 11, 1961. He was paid $650 and was entitled to receive 50 percent of anything over $1,700 in ticket receipts. This concert is noteworthy for ending a few minutes early after Dick Schmitz heard Berry say some things from the stage that he felt were inappropriate for the teen audience. (Courtesy of Dick Schmitz.)

This photograph from a late 1950s KAKC teen hop was featured in *Cashbox Magazine*, a record-industry trade publication. The Big 7 deejays are shown with recording artist Hershell Almond (far left). The deejays (in white jackets) are, from left to right, Dick Evans, Danny Dark, Dick Schmitz, and Harry Wilson. (Courtesy of Dick Schmitz.)

In 1963, crooner Bobby Vinton came to town to emcee a Miss Tulsa pageant at the Tulsa Municipal Theatre. A local orchestra backed him. Dick Schmitz recalls that the veteran musicians were skeptical of Vinton at first, since most of them had never heard of him. But Vinton won them over with his excellent arrangements. Pictured from left to right are Dick Hughes (president of Pepsi), Bobby Vinton, Cheryl Norris (Miss Tulsa, 1963), Dick Schmitz, and Phil Sherman. (Courtesy of Dick Schmitz.)

On October 29, 1961, Pres. John F. Kennedy travelled to Oklahoma for the ribbon-cutting ceremony for the Oachita National Park Road in Big Cedar. Clayton Vaughn, Harry Wilson, and Dick Schmitz flew down to southeastern Oklahoma to cover the event for KAKC. According to Wilson, Kennedy's trip was an effort to gain favor with influential US senator Robert S. Kerr. Because there was no power at the rural Oklahoma site, massive generators were flown in to beam the ceremony to the world. Schmitz recalls that, "after Kennedy finished his speech, he was leaving the stage when somebody remembered that they had never 'dedicated' the highway. So, he stopped, came back, and they then cut the ribbon. He had simply forgotten why he was there." Schmitz snapped this photograph, of Vaughn (left) and Wilson at the event, with the presidential podium in the background. (Courtesy of Dick Schmitz.)

After the ribbon-cutting ceremony at Big Cedar, Oklahoma, everyone, including all the press, went to the Kerr Ranch so the senator could show off his prize cattle to the president. This close-up of Kennedy was taken there. Clayton Vaughn recalls that Kerr sat in the bleachers as ranch hands paraded several head of cattle for review, including a big bull that was stopped directly in front of the president. Vaughn recalls that, when Kerr brought the commander in chief to view the animal up close, it "dropped a steaming pile of manure the diameter of a large dinner plate," which Kennedy proceeded to step in. According to Vaughn, the president was wearing black tassel loafers and, if he noticed, "gave absolutely no indication of it and continued his inspection." (Courtesy of Dick Schmitz.)

In 1962, S. Carl Mark, a Trenton, New Jersey businessman with experience both as a radio performer and owner, purchased KAKC. Mark's extensive career in broadcasting began in the 1930s in the New York City area, when he was in his early 20s. He worked as an announcer and also acted in radio plays. At WHK in Cleveland, Ohio, Mark emceed the nationally syndicated program *Mutual Goes Calling*, by the Mutual Broadcasting System. Mark owned WTTM in Trenton from 1948 to 1952, working with Ernie Kovacs, who, in the 1950s, became famous for his innovative television comedy. After selling WTTM and working for a decade in the family business in Trenton, Mark was ready to get back into the business he loved. According to Dick Schmitz, Mark's buying KAKC had a profound effect, essentially saving the station. "The previous owner had been spending some of KAKC's profits to support one of his less profitable stations," says Schmitz. (Courtesy of Mary Alice (Mark) Alexander.)

Here, S. Carl Mark, pictured in 1946, auditions teenagers to serve as panelists to discuss the problems of youth on the weekly radio program *It's Up to Youth* at radio station WOR in New York City. At that time, Mark was working in the Broadcast Department of the Al Paul Lefton advertising agency in New York. (Courtesy of Jon Mark and Mary Alice (Mark) Alexander.)

S. Carl Mark (back, left) and his wife, Patricia (front, left), were patrons of the arts in Tulsa, supporting several organizations, including the Tulsa Civic Ballet (which later became Tulsa Ballet Theater). This 1965 photograph shows the couple with KAKC general manager Robert J. Hoth (back, right) and his wife, Claudine (front right). (Courtesy of Jon Mark.)

The Mark family poses for their 1965 holiday card around the KAKC horseless surrey. S. Carl Mark, an amateur photographer, used a timer to snap this picture himself. Pictured are S. Carl Mark (far left), his wife, Patricia (second from right), and their five children, from left to right, Sarah, Mary Alice, Priscilla, Henry, and Jon. The signs on the vehicle read "ye olde KAKC Mobile News" and "ye olde KAKC Tulsa 970 24 Hours." (Courtesy of Mary Alice (Mark) Alexander.)

In 1963, KAKC moved into their own building at the Trade Winds Motor Hotel, Fifty-first Street and Peoria Avenue. Dick Schmitz played the first record from the new location ("Hello Mudduh, Hello Fadduh," by Allan Sherman) at 2:10 a.m. on August 29th. The record disappeared, and Schmitz did not see it again until 30 years later, when S. Carl Mark surprised him with it, framed and inscribed as being the first one played at the Trade Winds. (Courtesy of the author.)

The runaway success of the Beatles in the United States in early 1964 spawned the British music invasion. Many UK artists began having success on the US charts and set off on American tours. Nearly all of them played in Tulsa. The Dave Clark Five, known for their Beatles-esque hits, "Glad All Over," "Bits and Pieces," and "Can't You See That She's Mine," performed on December 2, 1964. Seen at right is the invitation that admitted entry into the private press party for the band, sponsored by KAKC at the Adams Hotel, just up the street from the Tulsa Civic Assembly Center where the group appeared that night. Below, at the press party, Dave Clark (second from right) is pictured with KAKC station owner S. Carl Mark's children and their friend Trimble Parlette (center). Jon Mark is on the left, and Mary Alice Mark is on the right. (Both, courtesy of Mary Alice (Mark) Alexander.)

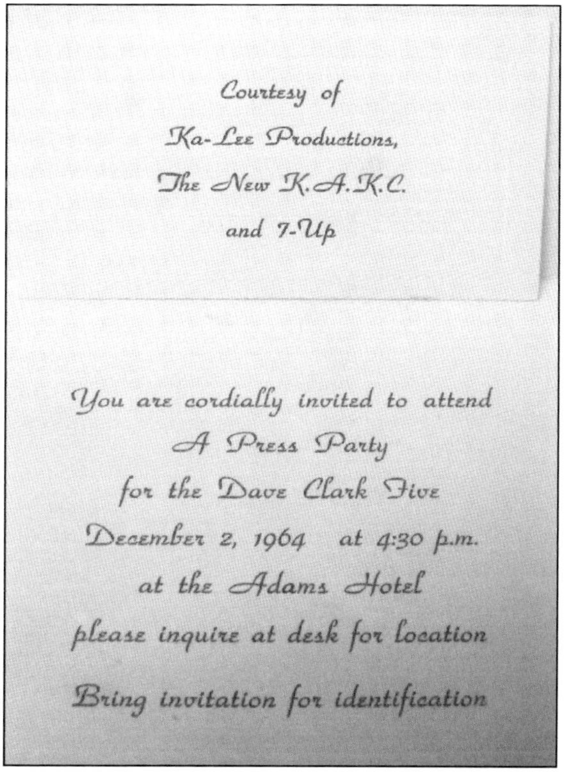

Courtesy of
Ka-Lee Productions,
The New K.A.K.C.
and 7-Up

You are cordially invited to attend
A Press Party
for the Dave Clark Five
December 2, 1964 at 4:30 p.m.
at the Adams Hotel
please inquire at desk for location
Bring invitation for identification

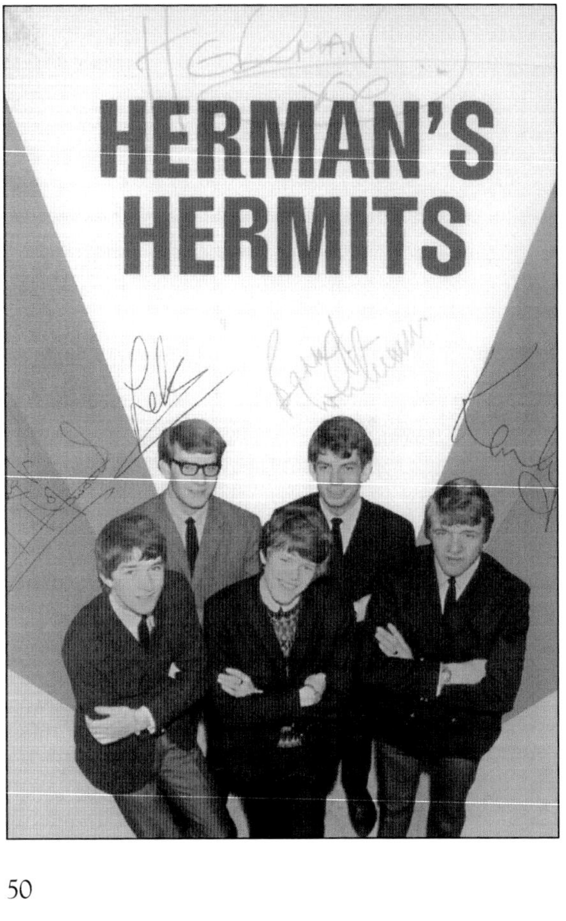

One of the most popular UK bands to invade the US charts, the Animals, played Tulsa on September 29, 1964, supporting their chart-topping "The House Of The Rising Sun." Before the KAKC-sponsored concert, the band relaxes poolside at the Trade Winds West with the Big 7 deejays. Pictured are, from left to right, (front row) Alan Price (keyboards), Eric Burdon (vocals), and Chas Chandler (bass); (second row) Harry Wilson, Dick Schmitz, Dick Ralston, and Gene Thomas. (Courtesy of Dick Schmitz.)

When British invasion band Herman's Hermits played the Tulsa Civic Assembly Center in a KAKC-sponsored concert, Dick Schmitz got the members to sign an official Herman's Hermits program. Inside, it states that the band gave their lead singer, Peter Noone, the nickname "Herman" because Noone reminded his bandmates of a character named Sherman from *The Rocky and Bullwinkle Show*. Noone's age at the time of this tour was just 17. His signature (signed as "Herman") is visible at the top of the program. (Courtesy of Dick Schmitz.)

In March 1964, with Tulsa and the rest of the nation in the throws of Beatlemania, KAKC Big 7 deejays Bob Brown and Dick Schmitz recorded a spoof of the Beatles song "From Me To You." Brown played guitar, and they both performed vocals. Calling themselves the Bugs, they played the song on the air once, just for fun. Then they started getting requests for it, which eventually led to several appearances, including one with the Tulsa Philharmonic Orchestra in concert. This photograph of the Bugs with Tulsa Philharmonic members, wearing tuxedos and Beatles wigs, appeared on the cover of the entertainment section of the *Tulsa Sunday World*. Brown, who went on to a career in television and became a correspondent on the ABC News program *20/20*, is the one with the guitar (second row, left). Schmitz is front and center, with outstretched hands. (Courtesy of Bob Brown.)

Beatlemania in Tulsa surely peaked with KAKC's "Spell 7 Up" contest, in which the 25 winners got to travel to see the Beatles in concert in Dallas. The first 25 listeners to spell out "Seven Up" with specially lettered bottle caps won expenses-paid trips to Dallas in a KAKC-chartered plane to attend the Fab Four's September 18, 1964, show at Dallas's Memorial Auditorium. Above, the contest winners pose on the tarmac with officials from Tulsa's 7-Up Bottling Company. Below, Harry Wilson interviews one of the excited winners. (Both, courtesy of John Durkee.)

Above, in a 1964 KAKC-sponsored concert, the Beach Boys play to an enthusiastic crowd at the Tulsa Civic Assembly Center. Below, Big 7 deejays Dick Schmitz (left) and Harry Wilson (center) assist the band on stage right before introducing them to the crowd. (Both, courtesy of Dick Schmitz.)

Perhaps the biggest rock-and-roll show KAKC sponsored at the Tulsa Civic Assembly Center was the Rolling Stones concert, during their *Satisfaction* tour. When they played the arena in November 1965, it was Dick Schmitz's job to attempt to keep the euphoric young fans in their seats. (Courtesy of Dick Schmitz.)

As the Beatles blasted from KAKC's control room, there was a totally different sound coming from the studio down the hall. In 1964, KAKC owner S. Carl Mark signed on KAKC-FM 92.9, which featured classical music and a weekly opera broadcast, with commentaries that Mark researched, wrote, and delivered himself. At first, the station only broadcast in the evenings from 6:00 p.m. to 11:00 p.m. Some of KAKC-AM's personnel split their time, also announcing classical tunes. Dick Schmitz is pictured in the classical studio. (Courtesy of Dick Schmitz.)

It is impossible to overstate the influence of the Beatles on popular music and youth culture. Their sound spawned many garage bands in the Tulsa area in the mid-1960s. KAKC supported that scene through the Battle of the Bands, a competition held in the towns around Tulsa, like Claremore and Collinsville. In each battle, two bands faced off for a chance to play in the finale, Battle of the Kings, at the Tulsa Civic Assembly Center. A frequent winner of those competitions, Rogues Five from Sand Springs, featured future Oklahoma Music Hall of Famer Jamie Oldaker. Above, the band performs outdoors at Miss Jackson's in Utica Square. Below, Rogues Five bandmates pose during the Summer of Love, 1967. From left to right are George "Pizza" Thomas (bass), Phillip Wilson (keyboards), I.J. Ganem (guitar, vocals), Jamie Oldaker (drums), and Randy Ess (guitar, vocals). (Both, courtesy of George Leslie Thomas.)

This 1960s publicity shot, taken in the wide-open spaces at Southern Hills Country Club, shows off the latest addition to the KAKC news fleet: Casey Bird-1, billed as "Tulsa's 1st Air Watch." Jon Mark (son of KAKC owner S. Carl Mark), who is sitting in the jeep on the left side of this photograph, recalls how hard it was to get that shot that day. The helicopter had to fly low enough to please the photographer, but when it did it kicked up a lot of wind and dust, making it difficult to get a clear shot. The man standing next to the KAKC horseless surrey and peering through a telescope is Hillis Bell Jr. A huge print of this photograph hung in the KAKC lobby for 15 years and is now in the home of Henry Mark. (Courtesy of Henry Mark.)

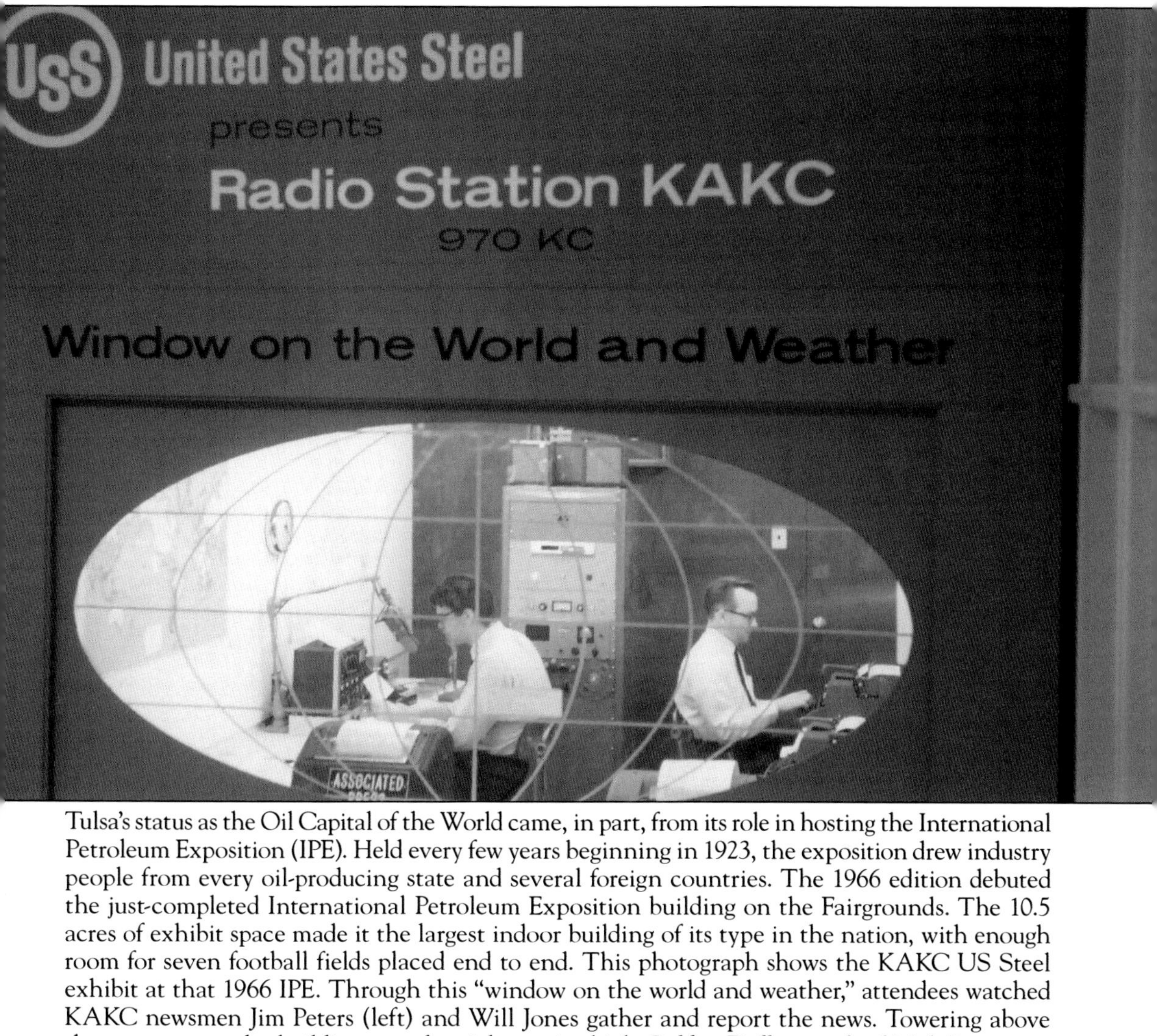

Tulsa's status as the Oil Capital of the World came, in part, from its role in hosting the International Petroleum Exposition (IPE). Held every few years beginning in 1923, the exposition drew industry people from every oil-producing state and several foreign countries. The 1966 edition debuted the just-completed International Petroleum Exposition building on the Fairgrounds. The 10.5 acres of exhibit space made it the largest indoor building of its type in the nation, with enough room for seven football fields placed end to end. This photograph shows the KAKC US Steel exhibit at that 1966 IPE. Through this "window on the world and weather," attendees watched KAKC newsmen Jim Peters (left) and Will Jones gather and report the news. Towering above the entrance to the building was the eight-stories-high *Golden Driller*, a gift of Mid-Continent Supply Company. (Courtesy of Mary Alice (Mark) Alexander.)

Pepsi-Cola Bottling Company and Safeway were two of KAKC's biggest advertising clients through the years. Above, this treasure hunt had a map with clues to the whereabouts of the treasure. The prize was one million Gunn Bros. stamps, which were redeemable for merchandise. At left, Vernell C. Wilson beams as she displays the groceries she gathered in 10 minutes as the winner of a Pepsi-Cola shopping spree. Fred Rowland (center), district manager of Safeway, is holding the cash register tape (which totals $891) along with R.H. "Dick" Hughes (right), president of Pepsi-Cola. Harry Wilson (back) phones in a report on the event to KAKC listeners. (Courtesy of Dick Schmitz.)

Oklahoma-headquartered Cities Service teamed up with KAKC on their new modern service station on the southwest corner of Twenty-first Street and Yale Avenue. According to KAKC's November-December 1964 newsletter, "the lighted sign, visible in this 1964 photograph, is the KAKC-operated 'Newscope,' which flashes to motorists throughout the day the latest news, weather and sports." (Courtesy of John Durkee.)

One of the first things S. Carl Mark did after purchasing KAKC in 1963 was move the station from downtown into new facilities at the Trade Winds Motor Hotel at Fifty-first Street and Peoria Avenue. That location became known as the Trade Winds West, since there were two other Trade Winds hotels in Tulsa. KAKC's offices and studios were on the second floor in their own building, with meeting rooms on the bottom level. (Courtesy of McFarlin Library/Tulsa World.)

8 KAKC—970 SECTION

Former KAKC DJ's Return to Fair

Danny Dark Gene Thomas Clayton Vaughn Don Kelly John Trotter Will Jones

Chris Lane Hillis Bell, Jr. Frank Lawrence Bob Brown

RETURN FOR EVENT—Ten former KAKC DJ's, who have moved to higher positions in radio, will return this weekend. They include Chris Lane of WJJD, Chicago; John Trotter, WJJD, Chicago; Hillis Bell Jr., KAKC sales manager; Gene Thomas, KRAV, Tulsa; Will Jones, KFMJ, Tulsa; Frank Lawrence, advertising agency, Tulsa; Bob Brown, KOTV, Tulsa; Clayton Vaughn, KOTV, Tulsa; Danny Dark, KLAC, Los Angeles; and Don Kelly, owner KUSH, Cushing.

The New KAKC management might do well to attach the title "College" to its present call letters, and begin issuing diplomas to personnel, upon completion of their "broad education" with the station.

That is the opinion of Robert J. Hoth, executive vice president and general manager of The New KAKC, as he looked back this week over the list of "alumni," and learned of their advancement in the field of radio bradcasting and communications.

Ten of these alumni will be back in Tulsa, as guests of the KAKC management, on Saturday and Sunday, to help celebrate the station's entry into the tenth year of "No. 1" rating for listenership in the Tulsa area. All had a part in helping to build the image of to-rating over nearly a decade. Numerous other "grads" will be unable to attend the observance.

The former staff personnel who will greet old friends and listeners on Saturday and Sunday at the Tulsa State Fair KAKC-Pepsi tent on the fairgrounds, will include the following personalities: Chris Lane, John Trotter, Hillis Bell Jr., Gene Thomas, Will Jones, Frank Lawrence, Bob Brown, Clayton Vaughn, Danny Dark and Don Kelly. They will be joined by present members of the "Big 7." Jerry Adams, formerly one of the New KAKC's most popular afternoon airmen, now a news announcer on KEDX-TV in Wichita Falls, Tex., will not be able to attend.

Those who have graduated to positions in other cities, will be flown back to Tulsa to join their fellow-alums during the two-day open house to be held at the fairgrounds—and to engage in some special receptions with staff members of KAKC.

It is estimated that teen-agers spend 12 billion dollars a year—and this does not include room, board, basic clothing, transportation and schooling.

In 1965, KAKC held its first reunion, of sorts, as 10 former staffers came back for an appearance at the Tulsa State Fair. The meet-and-greet event with listeners was held to celebrate the station's entry into their 10th year of No. 1 ratings. In the KAKC supplement to the *Tulsa World*, Robert J. Hoth, executive vice president and general manager of the station, compared the former employees to college students who had completed their broad education with the station and had gone on to advancement in the field of radio broadcasting and communications. The KAKC alums pictured in the article are, from left to right, (first row) Danny Dark, Gene Thomas, Clayton Vaughn, Don Kelly, John Trotter, and Will Jones; (second row) Chris Lane, Hillis Bell Jr., Frank Lawrence, and Bob Brown. (Courtesy of the *Tulsa World*.)

Robert Walker, pictured, began working at KAKC during his senior year at Tulsa Memorial High School. He started in the news department but got his big break one evening when the deejay for the 7:00 p.m. to midnight shift failed to show up. A favorite of Tulsa teens, he also hosted KOTV's *Dance Party*, a job that paid $50 per week, although Walker says he would have done it for free. (Courtesy of Dick Schmitz.)

KAKC staffers have respect and reverence for those at the station who mentored them. Both Jim Peters and Robert Walker say Big 7 deejay Roger Borden, pictured, helped them—in Walker's case, teaching him commercial production. Borden assisted Peters in getting a job at KAKC and later provided contacts for his acting aspirations. The Borden name was a familiar one to Tulsans through the family's chain of Borden's Cafeterias. (Courtesy of Dick Schmitz.)

DRINK Coca-Cola

KELI

FABULOUS FORTY SURVEY

TULSA'S TRUE WEEKLY MUSIC SURVEY

This Week	FOR WEEK ENDING AUGUST 13, 1965		Last Week
1.	SAVE YOUR HEART FOR ME	GARY LEWIS—Liberty	5
2.	WHAT'S NEW PUSSYCAT?	TOM JONES—Parrot	2
*3.	I'M HENRY THE VIII, I AM	HERMAN'S HERMITS—MGM	1
*4.	DON'T JUST STAND THERE	PATTY DUKE—U.A.	6
5.	YOU WERE ON MY MIND	WE FIVE—A&M	7
6.	DOWN IN THE BOONDOCKS	BILLY JOE ROYAL—Columbia	8
7.	I WANT CANDY	STRANGELOVES—Bang	10
8.	SATISFACTION	ROLLING STONES—London	4
9.	SUNSHINE, LOLLIPOPS AND RAINBOWS	LESLEY GORE—Mercury	11
10.	I LIKE IT LIKE THAT	DAVE CLARK FIVE—Epic	3
11.	THEME FROM A SUMMER PLACE	LETTERMEN—Capitol	13
12.	I GOT YOU BABE	SONNY AND CHER—Atco	34
13.	IT'S THE SAME OLD SONG	FOUR TOPS—Motown	14
14.	I'M A FOOL	DINO, DESI, AND BILLY—Reprise	24
15.	HOLD ME, THRILL ME, KISS ME	MEL CARTER—Imperial	16
16.	ALL I REALLY WANT TO DO	CHER/BYRDS—Imperial/Columbia	19
17.	TAKE ME BACK	LITTLE ANTHONY—DCP	20
18.	TO KNOW YOU	PETER AND GORDON—Capitol	25
19.	PRETTY LITTLE BABY	MARVIN GAYE—Tamla	22
20.	YES, I'M READY	BARBARA MASON—Arctic	15
21.	WHAT THE WORLD NEEDS NOW	JACKIE DESHANNON—Liberty	13
22.	CALIFORNIA GIRLS	BEACH BOYS—Capitol	30
23.	NOTHING BUT HEARTACHES	SUPREMES—Motown	—
24.	PAPA'S GOT A BRAND NEW BAG	JAMES BROWN—King	36
25.	ONE DYIN' AND A BURYIN'	ROGER MILLER—Smash	26
*26.	HELP	THE BEATLES—Capitol	—
27.	BABY I'M YOURS	BARBARA LEWIS—Atlantic	28
28.	YOU'D BETTER COME HOME	PETULA CLARK—Warner Bros.	29
29.	UNCHAINED MELODY/HUNG ON YOU	RIGHTEOUS BROS.—Phillies	32
30.	YOU TURN ME ON	IAN WHITCOMB—Tower	12
31.	TOO MANY RIVERS	BRENDA LEE—Decca	18
**32.	CARA MIA	JAY AND THE AMERICANS—U.A.	17
*33.	LOOKING THROUGH THE EYES OF LOVE	GENE PITNEY—Musicor	37
34.	MARIE	BACHELORS—London	9
35.	LIKE A ROLLING STONE	BOB DYLAN—Columbia	38
***36.	THE TRACKER	SIR DOUGLAS QUINTET—Tribe	—
37.	RIDE YOUR PONY	LEE DORSEY—Amy	39
38.	SINCE I LOST MY BABY	TEMPTATIONS—Gordy	—
39.	TRACKS OF MY TEARS	MIRACLES—Tamla	40
40.	NEW ORLEANS	EDDIE HODGES—Aurora	—

* PREVIOUS "RECORD OF THE WEEK"
** FORMER "PEEPLES PIK"
*** IN PERSON AUGUST 10th, CONTINENTAL ARENA
AUGUST 11th, BARTLESVILLE CIVIC CENTER
BOTH HOPS 9 TILL MIDNIGHT

Coke

RECORD OF THE WEEK
GIVE ALL YOUR LOVE TO ME
Gerry and the Pacemakers—Laurie

BILL KELLY
PETE KELLY
DALE KELLY
SAM KELLY
ROD KELLY
DAN KELLY

1430 the PULSE of TULSA!

During most of the 1960s and 1970s, Tulsa had two competing Top 40 radio stations in hot pursuit of the teen and young-adult audience. KTUL 1430 was sold in 1962 and became KELI 1430 under the ownership of Raymond Ruff. As can be seen on this KELI record survey from August 13, 1965, during this time, all of KELI's deejays used the last name of Kelly on the air. There were Bill, Pete, Dale, Sam, Rod, and Dan. Further confusing the name issue, one of KAKC's most popular deejays in the early 1960s was Kelly, along with his sidekick, Chauncey. (Courtesy of Wayne McCombs.)

The KELI studios and offices were in a circular building on the Tulsa Fairgrounds just east of Bell's Amusement Park. The KELI "Satellite Studios," as they were called, were originally part of the International Petroleum Exposition that was held for many years on that site. Once a year, KELI personnel found themselves in the middle of the Tulsa State Fair and opened their studios to public tours. (Courtesy of Mike Hardeman.)

Three

The Big 97

In 1966, KAKC's incredible 10-year run as Tulsa's No. 1 station ended when KELI-AM1430 beat it in the ratings. Scooter Segraves had been appointed program director only a few months earlier. "We simply piled on too many commercials. KELI was just easier to listen to and kicked our backsides," says Segraves.

After the ratings came out, KAKC owner S. Carl Mark and general manager Bob Hoth set out on a quest to do something to regain KAKC's momentum; they found help in an unlikely source. Hoth and Mark had been hearing about the astounding success of California consultant (and radio's new guru) Bill Drake. His revolutionary, streamlined system of Top 40 had taken stations in the biggest cities in the country, such as KHJ in Los Angeles, from the bottom of the ratings to No. 1.

Drake had unusual work habits for the time. Claiming he never had a good idea in an office, he worked from home by his pool and had special phone lines installed that allowed him to listen to any of his stations at any time. Drake was also choosy about whom he worked for. He personally consulted only a handful of stations, most of them in large cities on the East and West Coasts.

According to former Big 97 jock Beau Weaver, the timing was right when Mark and Hoth asked Drake and his partner Gene Chenault if they would bring their system of Top 40 to KAKC. According to Weaver, Drake and Chenault took it as an opportunity to prove that their methods would work in the Midwest and were "not just a big-city phenomenon."

Drake's system involved a specific set of rules that streamlined what the deejay did. Key elements were fewer commercials each hour and limited deejay talk. "It was almost like how haiku condenses great wisdom and beauty into just a few words. It taught the disc jockeys to do that kind of brevity," Weaver says.

Drake's top-secret entourage flew to Tulsa in February 1967 to train the KAKC deejays on his system. A new chapter in KAKC's history had begun, and "The Big 97" was born. The Big 7 deejays were now christened "the Big 97 jocks."

Bill Drake is one of the legendry figures in Top 40 radio, revolutionizing the way stations sounded with his streamlined "more music" system. Having Drake on KAKC's team in the late 1960s and early 1970s was a tremendous advantage for the station that paid off, bringing the station back to dominance in ratings. Above, Drake (left) confers with Big 97 jock Chris Martin in 1971. Martin says that working at KAKC was like getting a college education in broadcasting. (Courtesy of Chris Martin.)

The Drake KAKC logo is considered one of the most dynamic ever invented for radio. All of the stations Drake consulted used it, customized with their station's call letters and frequency. (Courtesy of Dial Global.)

It was February 1967 when California consultant Bill Drake gave KAKC's air sound a makeover. One aspect of the streamlined sound really jumped out at the listener: the short, a cappela jingles, or station identifiers between every song. These quick, vocal-only jingles like "more music KAKC" quickly became the standard in the radio industry. The jingles were written and sung by the Johnny Mann Singers, a seven-member Southern California vocal group who worked in movies, commercials, and television. They were also recording artists. The success of these jingles gave their leader, Johnny Mann, a whole other career that would span 50 years. Oldies stations around the country still use Mann's jingles today. This photograph, from a jingle session in Chatworth, California, features the group's 2005 lineup. Pictured are, from left to right, Bob Joyce (bass), Melissa Mackay (alto), Johnny Mann, Darlene Koldenhoven (soprano), Andy Waterman (engineer), Linda Harmon, (soprano), Randy Crenshaw (tenor/baritone) and Don Shelton (tenor). (Courtesy of Johnny Mann.)

In 1968, when Scooter Segraves left to become program director for Drake's station in Memphis (WHBQ), Lee Bayley became KAKC's program director. Bayley says one element that Drake's consultancy brought to the station was contests with bigger prizes. Under Drake, KAKC had the same exciting contests as his big stations in Los Angeles and San Francisco, although the prizes were adjusted for each individual station. At left, a Big 30 record survey features a key in the "Seven Car Sweepstakes," in which contestants entered for a chance to win their choice of America's seven grooviest cars. Below, Bayley promotes another new KAKC car giveaway. (Courtesy of Wayne McCombs.)

In this 1968 KAKC contest, listeners were instructed to answer their phones with the words "Think mink" for the chance to win a $600 mink stole. The phrase "Think Mink" was incorporated into surveys during the weeks of the contest. Below right, Scooter Segraves poses for a photograph with Corine Wooten, the first Think Mink winner. (All, courtesy of Wayne McCombs.)

KAKC'S "BIG 30" RECORDS IN GREATER TULSA

ISSUE NO. 16 ---PREVIEWED JUNE 7, 1967

LAST WEEK	THIS WEEK	TITLE	ARTIST	LABEL	WEEKS ON BIG 30
1	1	WINDY	The Association	Warner Bros.	5
3	2	TOO MANY FISH IN THE SEA	Mitch Ryder	New Voice	5
6	3	RESPECT	Aretha Franklin	Atlantic	5
7	4	HIM OR ME, WHAT'S IT GONNA BE	Paul Revere/The Raiders	Columbia	4
10	5	SHE'D RATHER BE WITH ME	The Turtles	White Whale	4
2	6	DO IT AGAIN, A LITTLE BIT SLOWER	Jon & Robin	Abnak	8
13	7	THE SOUND OF LOVE	The 5 Americans	Abnak	4
5	8	GROOVIN'	The Young Rascals	Atlantic	8
15	9	SOMEBODY TO LOVE	The Jefferson Airplane	RCA Victor	3
12	10	HAPPY JACK	The Who	Decca	4
9	11	SIX O'CLOCK	The Lovin' Spoonful	Kama Sutra	5
19	12	MIRAGE	Tommy James/The Shondells	Roulette	3
4	13	BLUE'S THEME	Davie Allen/The Arrows	Tower	7
29	14	SOCIETY'S CHILD	Janis Ian	Verve	2
17	15	GIRLS IN LOVE	Gary Lewis/The Playboys	Liberty	4
21	16	MY GIRL JOSEPHINE	Jerry Jaye	Hi	6
22	17	THE TRACKS OF MY TEARS	Johnny Rivers	Imperial	3
25	18	LIGHT MY FIRE	The Doors	Elektra	2
24	19	SAN FRANCISCO	Scott McKenzie	Ode	2
16	20	BOWLING GREEN	The Everly Brothers	Warner Bros.	6
8	21	I'VE GOT RHYTHM	The Happenings	B. T. Puppy	8
26	22	DON'T SLEEP IN THE SUBWAY	Pet Clark	Warner Bros.	3
23	23	SHAKE A TAIL FEATHER	James & Bobby Purify	Bell	3
30	24	NEW YORK MINING DISASTER, 1941	The Bee Gees	Atco	2
28	25	SEVEN ROOMS OF GLOOM	The 4 Tops	Motown	2
HB	26	DON'T BLAME THE CHILDREN	Sammy Davis Jr.	Reprise	1
HB	27	A LITTLE BIT O' SOUL	The Music Explosion	Laurie	1
HB	28	C'MON, MARIANNE	The 4 Seasons	Philips	1
HB	29	SUNDAY WILL NEVER BE THE SAME	Spanky/Our Gang	Mercury	1
HB	30	LET'S LIVE FOR TODAY	The Grass Roots	Dunhill	1

THE POPULARITY OF RECORDS LISTED HEREIN IS THE OPINION OF KAKC, BASED ON ITS SURVEY OF RECORD SALES IN TULSA CORRELATED WITH LISTENER REQUESTS.

Bill Drake reduced the size of KAKC's playlist from the Top 50 songs to 30, reasoning that anything more than that led to "playing too many songs that weren't really hits," according to Scooter Segraves. This Big 30 from June 7, 1967, shows "Windy" by the Association at No. 1. (Courtesy of Wayne McCombs.)

One of the best-remembered promotions during the Bill Drake era at KAKC was the holiday-season contest, "Christmas Wish." Listeners sent in their wishes, and KAKC teamed up with their advertisers to grant as many of them as they could. They did this popular promotion annually for several years, beginning in 1967. Big 97 jock Jim Peters is pictured on the *Big 30* survey with the details of the contest. (Courtesy of Wayne McCombs.)

At right, Big 97 jock Johnnie Laine and friends decorate the KAKC Christmas tree. Below, the KAKC Santas (from left to right) Tom Gordon, Bill O'Hara, Randy Castle, and Robert W. Walker solicit Christmas wishes. Program director Lee Bayley, who coordinated the Christmas Wish efforts, recalls one instance in which a young boy from an orphanage called in with a request. The boy explained that there were 12 children at the orphanage but only one bicycle, and he asked if they could have a second. For playback on the air, the announcer replied, "Bobby, we hear you. We agree that you need another bike. So we went to Oklahoma Tire and Supply and made a deal with them. But really, since there are 12 of you, don't you need 12 bikes? We'll be bringing them by this afternoon. Merry Christmas." (Both, courtesy of Wayne McCombs.)

Singer/songwriter and native Tulsan David Gates had a long association with KAKC that began in the late 1950s, when Dick Schmitz would hire Gates to back up artists who played KAKC's teen hops. When Gates's band, Bread, was getting started, the station played some of their early releases before they broke nationally with songs like "Make It with You" and "If." At left is a holiday card from Gates to KAKC. (Courtesy of Dick Schmitz.)

BIG 30
FROM 97/KAKC

Dig some of the Heavy Hits heard first-- EXCLUSIVELY-- on KAKC. . . . .

HEROES AND VILLAINS . . . . Beach Boys
A DAY IN THE LIFE . . . . Beatles
PLEASANT VALLEY SUNDAY . . Monkees
A WHITER SHADE OF PALE. Procol Harum
BABY YOU'RE A RICH MAN. . . Beatles
Windy . . . . Association

And many more, including these sounds heard ONLY ON KAKC

SOCIETY'S CHILD . . . . . . Janis Ian
LIGHT MY FIRE . . . . Doors
WHITE RABBIT . . . . . Jefferson Airplane
VALERIE . . . . Monkees
THENE FOR A NEW LOVE . . . Davy Jones
YOU KNOW WHAT I MEAN . . Turtles

THE BIG 97 is Oklahoma'S new music headquarters .. . where the heavy hits happen first.

One perk of KAKC's association with Bill Drake was access to music exclusives. "Drake was right next to the Beatles," says former Big 97 jock Jim Peters. "They would pull new Beatles songs right off the masters and send them to all the Drake stations. Sometimes, we would have them a couple of weeks before they were released to the rest of the country." A few KAKC exclusives are listed on this KAKC *Big 30* from 1967, including the Beatles' "A Day in the Life." (Courtesy of Wayne McCombs.)

Like his Will Rogers High School classmate David Gates, Leon Russell was a special friend of KAKC. Russell visited the station many times through the years and performed at KAKC-sponsored concerts. The station played Russell's releases like "Roll Away the Stone" and "Home Sweet Oklahoma," in addition to his national Top 40 chart hits. Pictured in this display from the KAKC exhibit at the Tulsa Historical Society are a Leon Russell album and other concert memorabilia. Also visible is an album by Teegarden & Van Winkle, the duo of drummer-vocalist Dave Teegarden and organist-vocalist Skip "Van Winkle" Knape, both Tulsans who achieved success after moving to Detroit and cutting the hit "God, Love and Rock and Roll" in 1970. At one time, Bob Seger was a member of the band. (Courtesy of the author.)

KOTV Channel 6's *Dance Party* was a weekly teen dance show featuring Tulsa rock-and-roll acts like Gene Crose and the Rockets in addition to the occasional national touring band. At alternate times, KAKC's Lee Bayley and Robert W. Walker hosted. Pictured on the left in this Big 30 survey from June 14, 1967, Bayley appears with a winner of a Paul Revere and the Raiders jacket given away on the TV show. After shortening their name to simply The Raiders, the band performs in Tulsa in 1968. In the Big 30 photograph below, Big 97 jocks Lee Bayley (back row, left) and Tom Gordon (back row, right) pose with the band and backstage-pass winners. (Courtesy of Wayne McCombs.)

Glen Campbell appears in a KAKC concert at the Civic Assembly Center in 1968. Campbell was at the peak of his chart success that year, thanks to a pair of songs written by Oklahoma native Jimmy Webb, "By the Time I Get to Phoenix" and "Wichita Lineman." The singer's *Glen Campbell Goodtime Hour* also debuted on television that year as a summer replacement show for the *Smothers Brothers Comedy Hour.* (Courtesy of Dick Schmitz.)

Throughout the years, KAKC employed part-time deejays who worked on the weekends and when the full-time staff went on vacation. One of the top practitioners of the part-time trade, Steve Suttle, worked at The Big 97 between 1967 and 1972. Suttle, pictured here in a KAKC studio, says the experience was like being in a fraternity: "To be 18 and part of that sound—which was then fresh, new, and innovative—was a real treat." (Courtesy of Steve Suttle.)

Former Big 97 jock Beau Weaver says Scooter Segraves's mind is not wired like ours, referring to Segraves's unique brand of humor. For example, the *Big 30* survey on the right features a drawing of the albino aardvarque, a character Segraves often referred to on the air. Below, Segraves juggles phone calls on a *Big 30* survey from 1967. Segraves says the highlight of working at KAKC was the summer of 1967. "We played the seven-minute "Light My Fire" by the Doors. I'd do my talk-up introduction, then haul butt out to the Tradewinds swimming pool, chugalug a Coors, do three minutes in the water, and still get back upstairs in time to towel off, slip back into clothes, and hit the "More Music" jingle out of that Doors classic." (Both, courtesy of Wayne McCombs.)

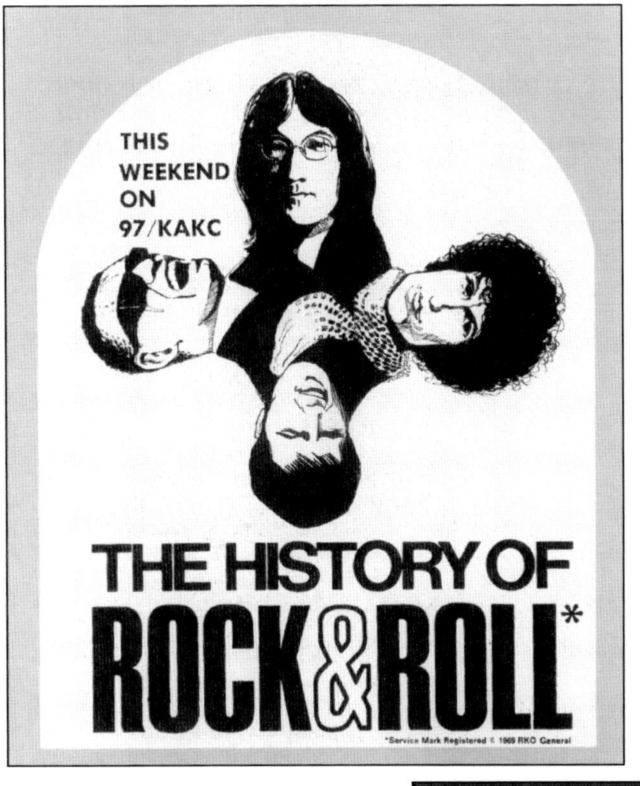

Program director Lee Bayley recalls the synergy of coordinating with the other stations consulted by Bill Drake, in cities like San Francisco, Los Angeles, San Diego, and Boston. One outcome of this collaboration was *The History of Rock and Roll*, a 50-hour documentary. For the original broadcast of this groundbreaking documentary in February 1969, Drake's office shipped the scripts and audio pieces to KAKC, and Bayley and Jim Peters narrated it themselves. Updated versions of the documentary heard on KAKC were narrated by Drake's Los Angeles voice talents or by Bill Drake himself. These *Big 30* surveys promote the original airing on February 28, 1969. (Courtesy of P. Casey Morgan.)

Of the documentary's impact, Lee Bayley says, "It really helped change the image of the radio station. It went from being a bunch of disc jockeys, all they do is yatter and play records, to people who were deep enough to produce a thing called *The History of Rock and Roll*," Bayley says. These two *Big 30* surveys promote the documentary and the contest that went along with it. (Both, courtesy of Wayne McCombs.)

Under Bill Drake's consultancy, as soon as one on-air contest would end, another would begin. On the Big 30 survey on the left, Robert W. Walker is not talking. While generally not a good strategy for a Big 97 jock, Walker is keeping silent on the secret of the KAKC Laugh-in contest. Below, Big 97 jock Randy Castle poses by another castle, The Camelot Hotel. Completed in 1965, Tulsa's all-electric hotel, was located just across the Interstate from KAKC, at I-44 and South Peoria Avenue. The once-majestic hotel was demolished in 2008. (Both, courtesy of Wayne McCombs.)

KAKC'S playlist reflected the times, ranging from Vietnam-protest songs like Edwin Starr's "War" (No. 2 on this *Big 30* survey) to songs about social issues like Marvin Gaye's "What's Going On." Although the station played them, KAKC's program director at the time, Lee Bayley, reminds that they never took a stand on an issue. "We were just there as a good source of music and to entertain a radio audience," Bayley says. (Courtesy of Wayne McCombs.)

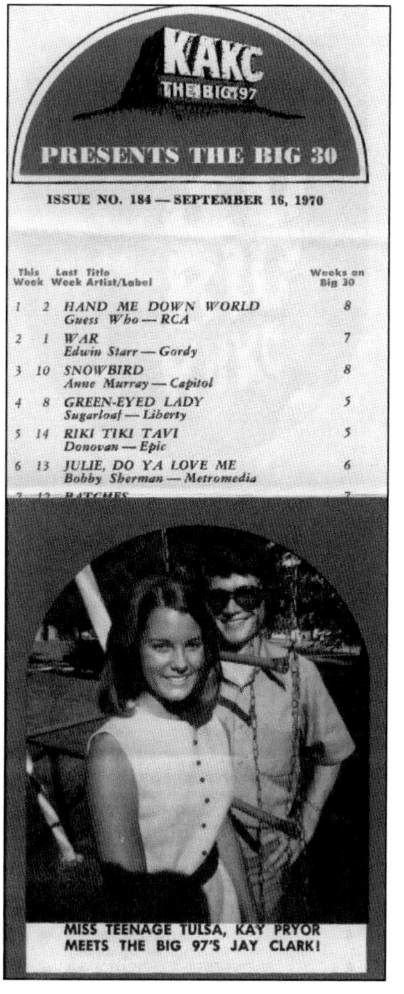

KAKC THE BIG 97

PRESENTS THE BIG 30

ISSUE NO. 184 — SEPTEMBER 16, 1970

This Week	Last Week	Title Artist/Label	Weeks on Big 30
1	2	HAND ME DOWN WORLD Guess Who — RCA	8
2	1	WAR Edwin Starr — Gordy	7
3	10	SNOWBIRD Anne Murray — Capitol	8
4	8	GREEN-EYED LADY Sugarloaf — Liberty	5
5	14	RIKI TIKI TAVI Donovan — Epic	5
6	13	JULIE, DO YA LOVE ME Bobby Sherman — Metromedia	6

MISS TEENAGE TULSA, KAY PRYOR MEETS THE BIG 97'S JAY CLARK!

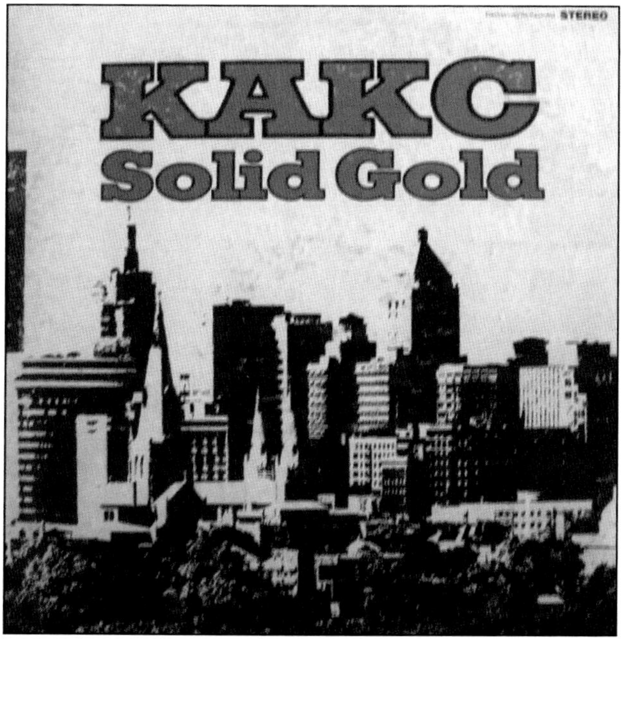

In 1969, the station released the *KAKC Solid Gold* album, a two-record set featuring 30 gold record tracks by various artists, including "Brown Eyed Girl," by Van Morrison, and "I Think We're Alone Now," by Tommy James & the Shondells—both of which were easy to license because they were owned by smaller record labels. The album's cover pictured the Tulsa skyline. (Courtesy of Tulsa Historical Society.)

Inside the double album's gatefold were photographs of the Big 97 jocks, labeled with their timeslots. Through the years, this album has become the most popular piece of KAKC memorabilia

for fans, even though most no longer own the equipment to play it on. (Courtesy of Tulsa Historical Society.)

The KAKC air staff was like a great college football team. When one player would graduate, another superstar-in-the-making would step into that position. When Scooter Segraves left KAKC for a while, Steve Hatley became Tulsans' choice for the drive home. Hatley left Tulsa in 1971 for Memphis and Minneapolis-St. Paul, before working on a highly rated morning show in Albuquerque, New Mexico. Below, Hatley drew the image on this Big 30 survey that promotes a 1970 countdown of the Top 40 songs of the 1960s. He died of injuries sustained in a motorcycle accident in New Mexico in 1984. (Both, courtesy of Wayne McCombs.)

During the 1960s, the Tulsa metropolitan area's population was hovering right around 500,000 and growing. A medium-sized city with an emphasis on the arts and culture, the opening of the Tulsa Civic Assembly Center in 1963 made the Oil Capital an attractive stop for big concert tours. Many of those shows were sponsored by KAKC. The list of artists who played this arena in the 1960s and 1970s is a who's who of popular music. In fact, nearly all of the British Invasion bands stopped in Tulsa on their US tours, with the exception of the Beatles, who came as close as Dallas. "KAKC was plugged in on the concert scene," recalls former Big 97 jock Jim Peters. "We had the Animals when 'House of the Rising Sun' was No. 1, we sponsored the Rolling Stones on their *Satisfaction* tour and the Doors, when 'Light My Fire' was No. 1." This photograph was taken from behind the stage of Glen Campbell's sold-out Civic Center concert in 1968. Attending a concert in this arena was a rite of passage for Tulsa teenagers during that era. (Courtesy Dick Schmitz.)

When Beau Weaver was a student at Bell Junior High in Tulsa, he used to call KAKC and request songs, talk to the deejays, and show up at personal appearances. "I was kind of the station's unofficial mascot," Weaver says. "I thought I was going to be the next KAKC deejay and because I didn't know it wasn't possible, I eventually became one." Weaver is pictured here on a *Big 30* survey. (Courtesy of Wayne McCombs.)

In the late 1960s, Big 97 jock Tom Gordon served as music director, the person who decides which songs are added to the playlist. Jim Peters says Gordon introduced Tulsans to Jimi Hendrix, Cream, Led Zeppelin, and Janis Joplin, as well as a host of black artists including Wilson Pickett, Otis Redding, Etta James, James Brown, and Aretha Franklin. Gordon signed off his show every day with the phrase "and don't forget to boogie!" Gordon passed away in July 2000. (Courtesy of Wayne McCombs.)

When former Big 97 jocks Beau Weaver and Robert W. Walker got together to talk about their KAKC days, Weaver said, "those of us who grew up in Tulsa have cultural touchstones that we all share: Bell's Amusement Park, Boots drive-in, cruising Brookside, greasers and soshs, Bama Pies, Big Bill and Oom-A-Gog, Lee and Lionel, Mazeppa, and KAKC. And we got to work there!" (Courtesy of Wayne McCombs.)

Several KAKC alums went on to do commercial voiceover work. Dick Schmitz's voice could be heard around the country for 40 years from his Irving Productions in Tulsa. Danny Dark became the voice of NBC television and was heard on commercials for Budweiser's "This Bud's for You" campaign and Starkist Tuna's "Sorry Charlie" spots. Randy Brown, also known as "Bob Scott," is the "station voice" of radio stations. Beau Weaver's voiceover credits include *Jimmy Kimmel Live!* Pictured here is the slate for a Beau Weaver voiceover. (Courtesy of Beau Weaver.)

Many KAKC-sponsored rock concerts had their own promotional posters, which are now quite collectable. The two posters above, from the Tulsa Historical Society's collection, advertise shows for Three Dog Night and Jimi Hendrix. Hendrix played Tulsa's Civic Assembly Center on June 7, 1970, just three months before his death. (Courtesy of the author.)

The *Big 30* survey for the week of Thanksgiving 1968, pictured left, promotes an upcoming concert by Vanilla Fudge. The psychedelic rock band had the No. 4 hit on the *Big 30* that week with "Take Me For A Little While." The band had an even bigger hit the previous year with a cover of the Supremes' classic "You Keep Me Hanging On." (Courtesy of Wayne McCombs.)

As part of his duties as program director, Lee Bayley was responsible for the concept and shooting of the photograph that appeared each week on the *Big 30* survey. Most often, it was one or more of the Big 97 jocks placed in some kind of fun scenario. One of the more creative ones, in the days before Photoshop, features an eight-stories-tall Lee Bayley at eye level with the *Golden Driller.* (Courtesy of Wayne McCombs.)

This stylish studio photograph from a 1970 *Big 30* survey shows four of the Big 97 jocks along with a promotional blurb about their current contest, the KAKC "Black Box." Pictured are, from left to right, Tom Gordon, Jim Peters, Dan Stone, and Randy Castle. (Courtesy of P. Casey Morgan.)

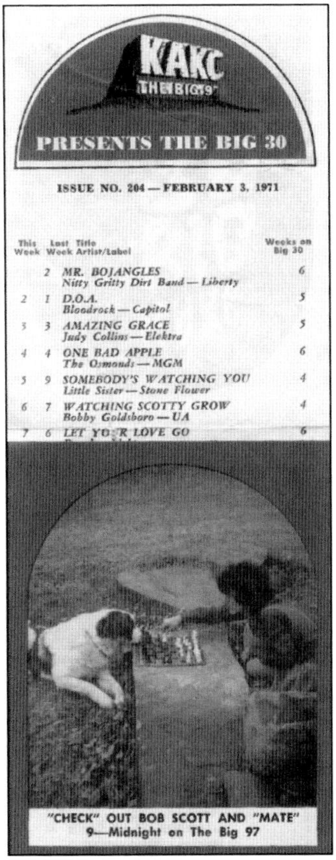
KAKC THE BIG 97

PRESENTS THE BIG 30

ISSUE NO. 204 — FEBRUARY 3, 1971

This Week	Last Week	Title Artist/Label	Weeks on Big 30
	2	MR. BOJANGLES Nitty Gritty Dirt Band — Liberty	6
2	1	D.O.A. Bloodrock — Capitol	5
3	3	AMAZING GRACE Judy Collins — Elektra	5
4	4	ONE BAD APPLE The Osmonds — MGM	6
5	9	SOMEBODY'S WATCHING YOU Little Sister — Stone Flower	4
6	7	WATCHING SCOTTY GROW Bobby Goldsboro — UA	4
7	6	LET YOUR LOVE GO	6

"CHECK" OUT BOB SCOTT AND "MATE"
9—Midnight on The Big 97

Randy Brown, a.k.a. "Bob Scott," worked at KAKC from 1970 through 1972. His Saint Bernard, Freedom, appears with him on the KAKC *Big 30* survey at left. Brown says Freedom had a special way of "christening" each radio station control room that Brown worked in, including KAKC's, in which he is pictured below. After Tulsa, Brown (and Freedom) moved on to Dallas and Houston, where he worked under the air name Christopher Haze. (Left, courtesy of Wayne McCombs; below, courtesy of Randy Brown.)

Tulsa native David Gates achieved national success in the early 1970s when his band, Bread, had a string of soft rock hits. In this 1970 survey image, Gates (center) visits with Big 97 jocks Lee Bayley (left) and Tom Gordon (right) while "Make It with You" is riding high on the Big 30 chart. (Courtesy of Wayne McCombs.)

As 1968 turned into 1969, the Big 97 jocks wished their listeners "Happy New Year" on the Big 30 survey. Seen here from left to right are (first row) Steve Suttle; (second row) Tom Gordon, and Robert W. Walker; (third row) Dave Jones, Lee Bayley, Bill O'Hara, and Jim Peters. (Courtesy of Wayne McCombs.)

Big 97 jock Chris Martin poses in front of the sign on the outside of the KAKC building at the Trade Winds West, Fifty-first Street and South Peoria Avenue. This sign was on the building's north side, facing Interstate 44. (Courtesy of Wayne McCombs.)

The unsung heroes of KAKC, the office staff, pose for this Big 30 Survey during Oscar nomination season in early 1970. Pictured from left to right are (first row) Charlene Boyd (receptionist), unidentified, Pat Bissey (secretary to S. Carl Mark), and Martha Stewart (copywriter); (second row) unidentified, Sharon Watkins (continuity director), unidentified, Wes Stegeman (salesman), unidentified, and Phil Sherman (salesman/promotion manager). (Courtesy of the author.)

In the late 1960s, listeners who sent in their names, addresses, and birthdates would receive this birthday card from KAKC. The outside of the card features a drawing by an unidentified artist, and inside are printed signatures of Big 97 jocks Lee Bayley, Randy Castle, Bill O'Hara, Dan Stone, Jim Peters, Tom Gordon, and Bobby Otis. The author received this one on his 16th birthday. (Courtesy of the author.)

The two photographs on this page are from a bike-riding event, described on the April 26, 1972, record survey as a warm-up for the Walk for Mankind, which would take place on May 6. Above, on bicycles are left to right, Big 97 jocks Johnnie Laine, Dave Corbitt, Steve Hatley and Simon Trane. Below, according to the survey, several bike-hikers pose with the jocks at the KAKC mobile studio. (Both, courtesy of Mary Alice (Mark) Alexander.)

The Walk For Mankind was an annual event in which participants got sponsors to pledge a certain amount of money for every mile they walked. The proceeds benefitted humanitarian efforts in Central America. KAKC took their mobile studio out to the very first one on May 6, 1972. A group of walkers peer into the KAKC mobile studio during the event. (Courtesy of Mary Alice (Mark) Alexander.)

Gailard Sartain, a.k.a. Mazeppa Pompazoidi, amassed a cult following on Tulsa television in the early 1970s. The *Uncanny Film Festival and Camp Meeting* featured Sartain and his cast of characters, including Gary Busey as Teddy Jack Eddy and Jim Millaway as Sherman Oakes, doing skits while hosting a late-night movie every Saturday night. After the show's TV run, first on KOTV Channel 6 and then on KTUL Channel 8, Sartain (center) and friends brought their act to KAKC on Saturday nights from 11:00 p.m. to 1:00 a.m., changing the name to the *Unfilmy Can Festival*. (Courtesy of Wayne McCombs.)

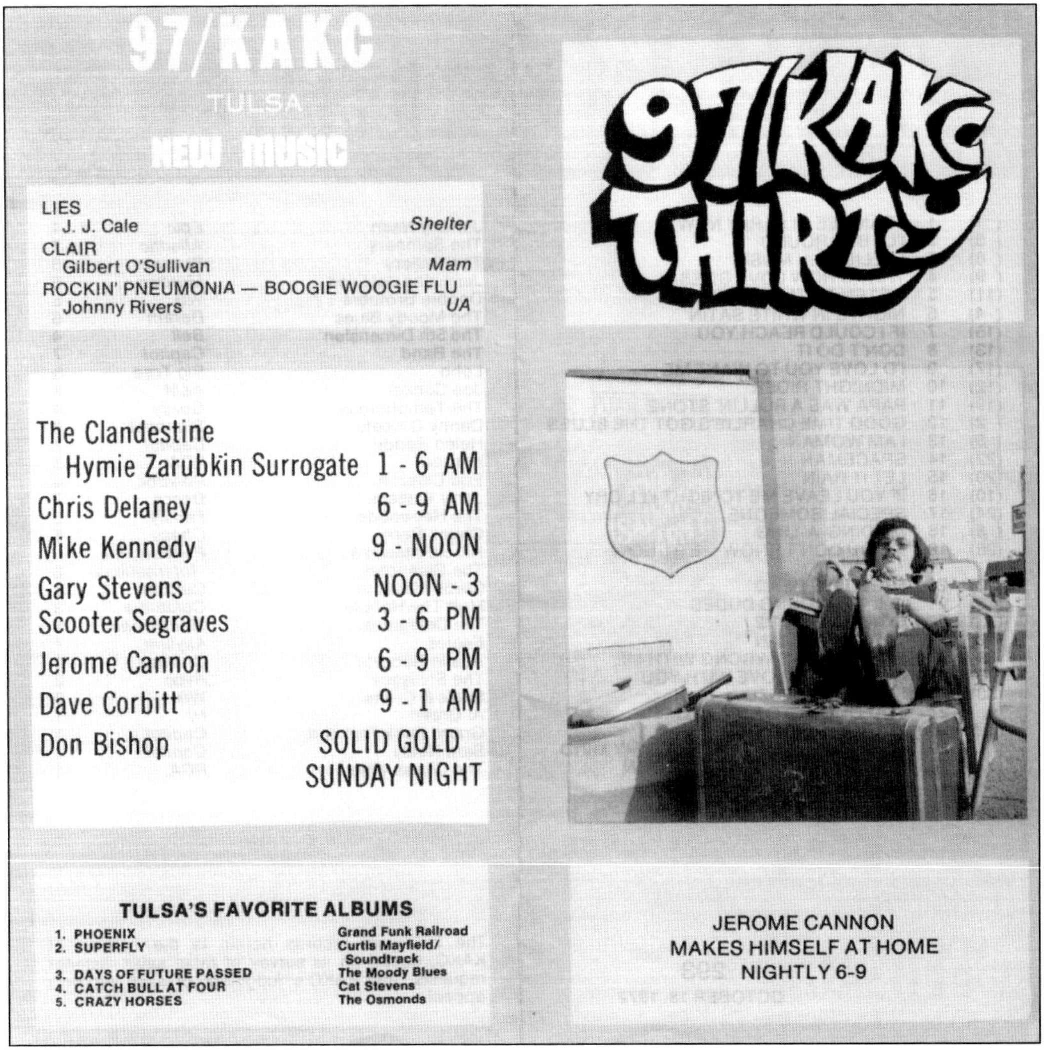

97/KAKC
TULSA
NEW MUSIC

LIES
J. J. Cale — *Shelter*
CLAIR
Gilbert O'Sullivan — *Mam*
ROCKIN' PNEUMONIA — BOOGIE WOOGIE FLU
Johnny Rivers — *UA*

The Clandestine Hymie Zarubkin Surrogate	1 - 6 AM
Chris Delaney	6 - 9 AM
Mike Kennedy	9 - NOON
Gary Stevens	NOON - 3
Scooter Segraves	3 - 6 PM
Jerome Cannon	6 - 9 PM
Dave Corbitt	9 - 1 AM
Don Bishop	SOLID GOLD SUNDAY NIGHT

97/KAKC THIRTY

TULSA'S FAVORITE ALBUMS

1. PHOENIX	Grand Funk Railroad
2. SUPERFLY	Curtis Mayfield/ Soundtrack
3. DAYS OF FUTURE PASSED	The Moody Blues
4. CATCH BULL AT FOUR	Cat Stevens
5. CRAZY HORSES	The Osmonds

JEROME CANNON
MAKES HIMSELF AT HOME
NIGHTLY 6-9

This *97/KAKC Thirty* record survey from 1972 pictures Jerome "Stone" Cannon and also includes the on-air lineup. The deejay listed for 1:00 a.m. to 6:00 a.m. could be a creation of afternoon deejay Scooter Segraves, who had recently returned to KAKC. Notably, Don Bishop is listed as hosting the city's first bona fide oldies show, *Solid Gold Saturday Night*. (Courtesy of Wayne McCombs.)

Four

The Rockin' 97

Just as the 1950s brought changes that led to the development of Top 40 radio on AM, the 1970s ushered in a new set of circumstances that would eventually lead to AM music radio's demise.

In Tulsa radio, the 1970s had a split personality. As the decade began, it was still an AM radio world. KAKC, riding high from its consulting from Bill Drake, was No. 1 with all listeners and held a 25 percent share of the audience. KRMG-AM740, with its middle-of-the-road, easy listening format, was No. 2, with 19 percent.

But advances in recording techniques and home stereo equipment were giving consumers a higher-quality listening experience. As album sales boomed, stereo, with its separate channels, was becoming the norm, and listening to music on AM's staticky single channel paled in comparison. When AM/FM radios became standard in cars, FM broadcasters finally could reach the audience they needed to become profitable.

New formats like album rock and beautiful music were emerging on FM in Tulsa on KMOD 97.5 and KWEN 95.5, respectively. FM 96 KRAV, literally waiting in the wings for 15 years, started surging by mid-decade with its adult contemporary soft rock sound. By 1978, KAKC would have additional competition on FM when KWEN 95.5 switched to Top 40, as did KTFX 103.3.

For KAKC, 1973 brought a change in consultants; a new name (the Rockin' 97); and a new program director, Gary "Ono" Stevens. The on-air line up during that era included Mike "Morning Mouth" McCarthy, Gary "Ono" Stevens, Charlie Derek, Scooter Segraves, and Denver Foxx. Collectively, they gave Tulsans many good reasons to keep listening to their music on AM.

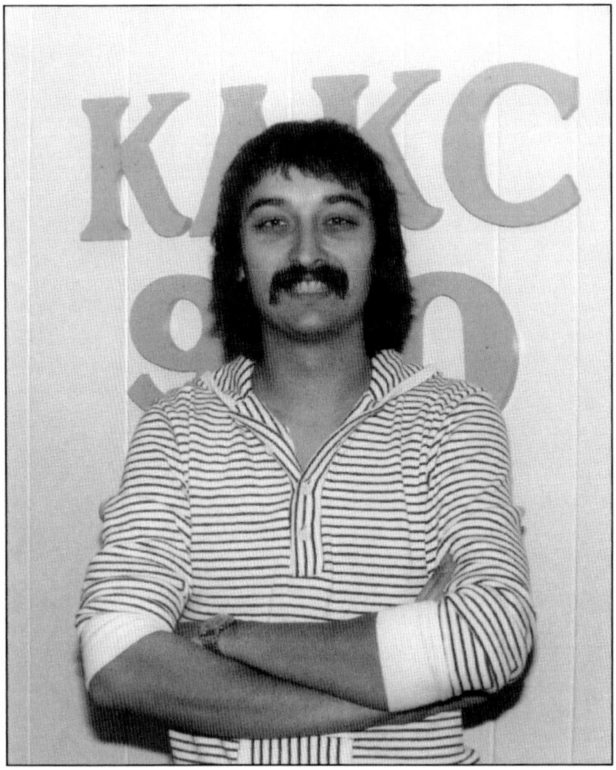

When Mike "Morning Mouth" McCarthy came to KAKC in June 1974, one of the first things he and his wife, Barbara, experienced was the June 8th tornado. It caused major damage to Tulsa's Brookside neighborhood, a few blocks from the KAKC studios. The storm also knocked most of the Tulsa radio stations off the air, including KAKC. Using generator power, the station got back on the air the next day to report on the damage. (Courtesy of Mike McCarthy.)

Henry Mark, son of KAKC owner S. Carl Mark, is pictured inspecting the fallen KAKC radio tower from the June 8th storm. Henry is standing behind the concrete base on which the tower had been mounted, and the severed bottom end of the tower is resting on the fence at the right. The bent wreckage can be seen extending off into the distance. (Courtesy of Mary Alice (Mark) Alexander.)

Gary "Ono" Stevens worked at KAKC from 1971 to 1975, becoming the program director in 1973. During this period, KAKC had dropped their affiliation with Bill Drake and were being consulted by Drake protégé Paul Drew. This era would see the station take on-air contesting to new heights as well as continuing its strong community involvement. Stevens also hired the first female deejay in the station's history, Sunny Ray. (Courtesy of Gary Stevens.)

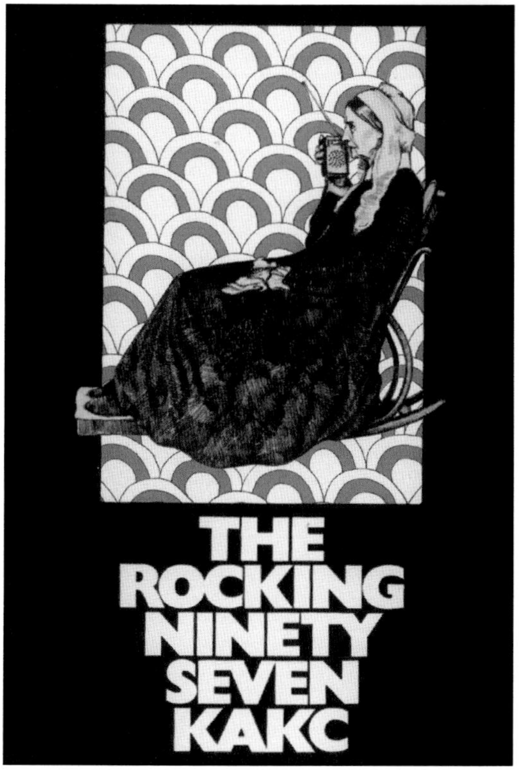

The first move with Paul Drew as consultant was a name change to the Rockin' 97. "It was in order to tip the scale just a little from pop to rock, given the emerging competition on FM," says KAKC program director Gary "Ono" Stevens. With that change, the station adopted a fun new logo that featured an elderly woman in a rocking chair listening to a transistor radio. (Courtesy of Wayne McCombs.)

Pictured here is the KAKC Terrific Turtle Race at Mall 31, around 1976, with Mike McCarthy emceeing. McCarthy says that, generally, around 500 KAKC fans would show up to events like this one. (Courtesy of Mike McCarthy.)

KAKC continued to maintain a basketball team that played area schools and other organizations. The mid-1970s incarnation of the team was called the KAKC Bumbling Basketball Boogie. According to Mike McCarthy, they never won a game. Pictured here are, from left to right, Captain Fantastic, Stan Hopkins, Mike McCarthy, and Gary "Ono" Stevens. (Courtesy of Mike McCarthy.)

Although started by KRMG AM740, the Great Raft Race became an event for all media and for all of northeastern Oklahoma each Labor Day weekend. Kasey Jones and Mike McCarthy ready the KAKC raft for the 10-mile float on the Arkansas River, which started at Sand Springs River City Park and finished along the River Parks in Tulsa. (Courtesy of Mike McCarthy.)

The Rockin' 97 deejays and their wives are pictured at the station Christmas party in 1974. From left to right are (first row) Debbie Derrick, Lois Fantastic, Lindy Hopkins, and Barbara McCarthy; (second row) Mike McCarthy, Michelle "Ono" Stevens, Gary "Ono" Stevens, Stan Hopkins, and Scooter Segraves; (third row) and Captain Fantastic. (Courtesy of Mike McCarthy.)

Back before plastic was prevalent, there was the KAKC Supercard. It was a joint promotion between the KAKC sales and programming departments. This plastic card was good for discounts at music stores and other merchants who advertised on the station. In a feature article about KAKC's upcoming 20th anniversary, the April 16, 1975, *Tulsa Tribune* reported that 35,000 Tulsans already had a KAKC Supercard "with a waiting list as long as your arm."

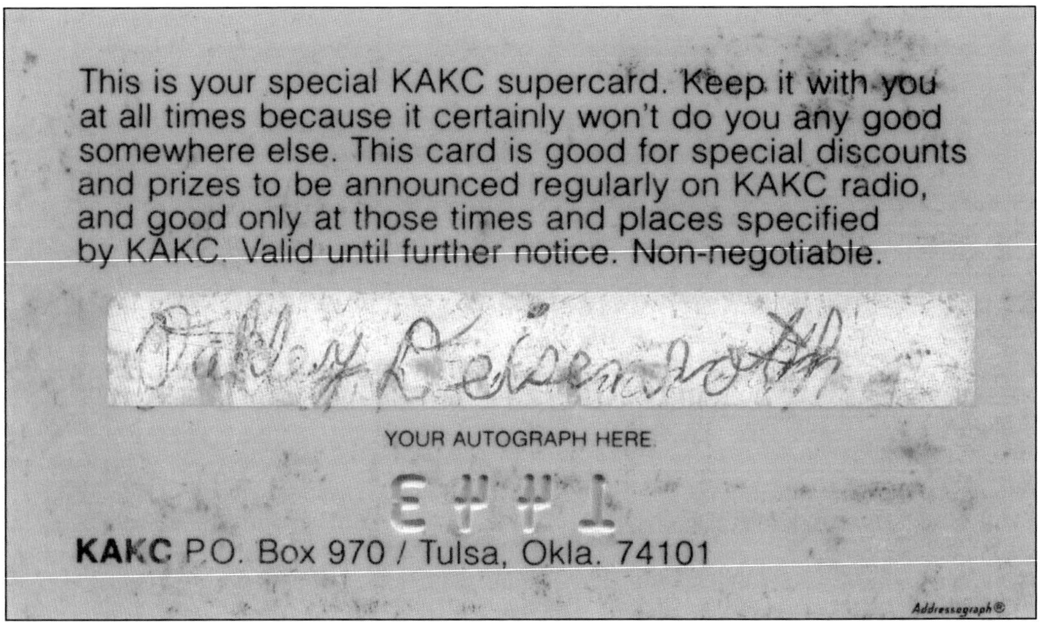

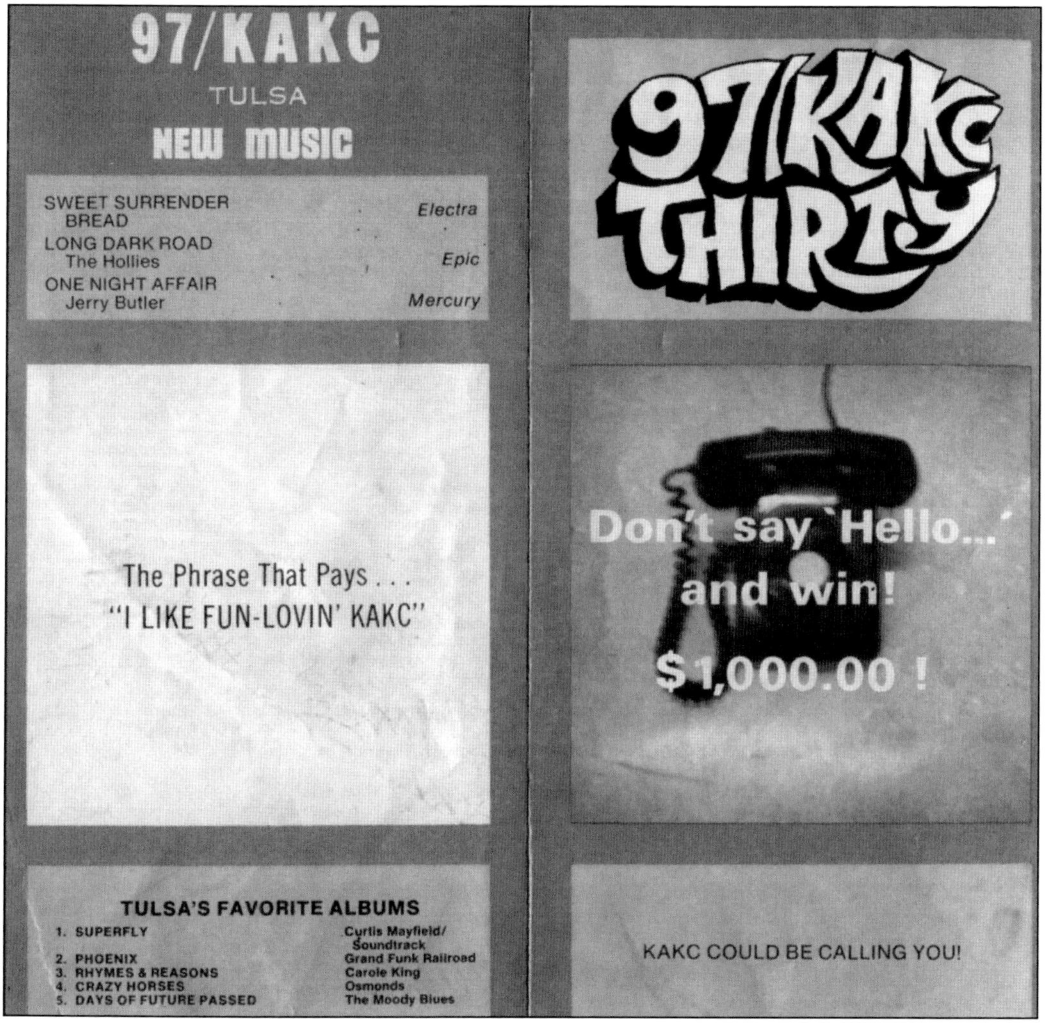

One of the most memorable Rockin' 97 contests is described on this 97 KAKC Thirty survey. The KAKC deejays called residences in northeastern Oklahoma throughout the day, and, since the phone calls were placed off the air, listeners never knew if or when they might occur. If listeners answered with the phrase "I like fun-lovin' KAKC," they would win a clean, crisp, new $1,000 bill. After the station gave away a few $1,000 bills, for the finale, they increased the cash prize to $10,000, an amount that inspired many Tulsans to temporarily change their phone-answering habits. (Courtesy of Wayne McCombs.)

Mike "Morning Mouth" McCarthy had a specific way of warming up, starting each show by saying, "it's six o'clock and I am your fab gear super-psychedelic boss every major market electric super freak-out, totally awesome rock-and-roll disc jockey. Today with cheap thrills, hot flashes, the McCarthy meter, the lunch menu, and lots more stuff." In the image above, McCarthy is seen at the first-annual Roy Clark Celebrity Golf Tournament at Cedar Ridge Country Club. Below, he is pictured hosting the legendary Rockin' 97 Bikini Contest at the KAKC Fourth of July Riverparks Festival Main Stage, around 1975. (Courtesy of Mike McCarthy.)

In 1975, the station celebrated the beginning of its 20th year as a Top 40 station. To commemorate this milestone, they constructed a temporary storefront studio at Southland Shopping Center at the southeast corner of Forty-first Street and Yale Avenue. The deejays did their shows from this studio for an entire week. The control room had a window, allowing listeners to peek in. Above, Charlie Derek is photographed doing his shift from the Southland studio. (Courtesy of Mike McCarthy.)

This looks like a media football team, but it is actually a promotion for Downtown Tulsa Unlimited (DTU), an event celebrating the end of vertical construction for the brand new hotel at the Williams Center in downtown Tulsa. These media men each tried to kick a field goal, and, as participant Mike McCarthy recalls, they all missed. Pictured here are, from left to right, unidentified, Jerry Webber (Channel 2), John Erling (KRMG), Charlie Derek (KAKC), and Mike McCarthy (KAKC). (Courtesy of Mike McCarthy.)

John Durkee is a veteran Tulsa radio news anchor and news director. In October 1978, however, he had been KAKC's news director for only a few months when owner S. Carl Mark called Durkee into his office. Durkee, pictured in 2012 in his KWGS 89.5 studio, was certain that he was about to be fired. Instead, Mark told him of his plans to change KAKC's format from Top 40 to easy listening. Mark asked Durkee to stay on, swearing him to secrecy about the coming changes. After 22 years as a Top 40 station, the end came at 12:00 noon on January 1, 1979. Mark delivered the announcement live after the playing of Heart's "Dreamboat Annie." The next song played was by Frank Sinatra. As Durkee recalls, "There had been no indication to the listeners that the format would change. The phones exploded with complaints. It was over." (Courtesy of John Durkee.)

Five

The Record Surveys

From Top 40's inception in the 1950s, counting down the top survey songs was a draw for listeners. KAKC started issuing its weekly printed Top 50 survey in the late 1950s, discontinuing the list in the latter half of the 1970s when interest in 45-rpm singles started to wane.

This chapter covers the various styles of the KAKC survey through the years. Former KAKC program director Dick Schmitz recalls compiling the Top 50 song list by collecting information from record shops (in particular, Bill's "T" Records), national chart rankings in *Cashbox* and *Billboard*, and record distributors (whose data, Schmitz says, they "took . . . with a grain of salt since [distributors] tended to hype the songs that weren't selling as well").

These weekly record surveys were available at record shops throughout northeastern Oklahoma and in the record departments of stores like JC Penney, Woolworth's, Sears, and TG&Y. Many record departments stocked their shelves according to the KAKC survey.

Picking up the KAKC list was a weekly ritual for many listeners, who would then use it as a guide to purchase their favorite 45-rpm singles. The price of a single record in 1968 at JC Penney in Southland was 74¢.

As it turns out, these record surveys held up better than the records themselves. Scratchy 45s and the equipment to play them on (including those adapters that went in the center hole) have largely been discarded. These KAKC surveys, printed on paper stock that has held up remarkably well, are now cherished collectibles. They are a window into the memories of youth and a radio station that touched so many lives.

TOP 50

the new KAKC

970 on your dial.

THE OFFICIAL RECORD PULSE OF TULSA – BASED ON SALES, JUKE BOX PLAYS AND YOUR REQUESTS TO THE NEW KAKC . . . . .

Compiled and Distributed free by KAKC.

WEEK OF December 8 1958

NEW KAKC PIC-HIT OF THE WEEK -- PETER GUNN -- RAY ANTHONY -- CAPITOL
NEW KAKC PIC-PAIR ALBUMS -- THE VERY THOUGHT OF YOU-- NAT KING COLE -- CAPITOL AND FANCY MEETING YOU HERE-- BING CROSBY & ROSEMARY CLOONEY -- RCA VICTOR

•MUSIC AND NEWS 24 HOURS A DAY•

	TITLE	LAST WEEK	
1.	The Chipmunk Song -- The Chipmunks	41	Liberty
2.	Smoke Gets In Your Eyes -- The Platters	1	Mercury
3.	I Cried A Tear -- LaVern Baker	2	Atlantic
4.	Problems -- The Everly Brothers	3	Cadence
5.	The Fool And The Angel -- Bobby Helms	8	Decca
6.	One Night -- Elvis Presley	5	RCA
7.	Rockhouse -- Ray Charles	6	Atlantic
8.	Caravan, Part II -- Cozy Cole	7	Felsted
9.	Love You Most Of All -- Sam Cooke	9	Keen
10.	Lonely Teardrops -- Jackie Wilson	25	Brunswick
11.	Ain't I The Lucky One -- Marty Robbins	26	Columbia
12.	Beep Beep -- The Playmates	4	Roulette
13.	Merry Christmas, Baby --Chuck Berry	--	Chess
14.	It's Just About Time -- Johnny Cash	33	Sun
15.	To Know Him Is To Love Him -- The Teddy Bears	14	Dore
16.	Save My Soul -- Jack Scott	38	Carlton
17.	Oh Yeah! Uh Huh! -- Mickey & Sylvia	27	RCA
18.	Heartbeat -- Buddy Holly	15	Coral
19.	She Knows How To Rock -- Little Richard	16	Specialty
20.	The Worrying Kind -- Tommy Sands	17	Capitol
21.	Tom Dooley -- Kingston Trio	18	Capitol
22.	Whole Lotta Loving -- Fats Domino	10	Imperial
23.	Sweet Little Rock And Roll -- Chuck Berry	12	Chess
24.	That's Why I Cry -- Buddy Knox	45	Roulette
25.	My Happiness -- Connie Francis	47	MGM
26.	My Babe -- Dale Hawkins	19	Checker
27.	My Baby's Gone -- Johnnie & Joe	21	Chess
28.	Keep A Driving -- Chuck Willis	20	Atlantic
29.	Topsy -- Cozy Cole	11	Love
30.	Big Bopper's Wedding -- The Big Bopper	13	Mercury
31.	No One Knows -- Dion and The Belmonts	28	Laurie
32.	I Ain't Hurtin -- Sarah Vaughn	30	Mercury
33.	You're Making A Fool Out Of Me -- Jimmy Newman	32	MGM
34.	Drum Village -- Earl Palmer	34	Capitol
35.	Go Chase A Moonbeam -- Jerry Vale	39	Columbia
36.	Peek-A-Boo -- The Cadillacs	40	Josie
37.	When I Speak Your Name -- Frankie Laine	46	Columbia
38.	One Great Love -- The Five Keys	--	Capitol
39.	That Old Black Magic -- Louis Prima & Keely Smith	29	Capitol
40.	Funny -- Jesse Belvin	--	RCA
41.	Flat Tire -- Del Vikings	--	Mercury
42.	Hideaway -- The Four Esquires	24	Paris
43.	The M Squad Theme -- Count Basie	42	Roulette
44.	The Diary -- Neil Sedaka	43	RCA
45.	We Kiss In A Shadow -- Vic Damone	48	Columbia
46.	Mama, He Treats Your Daughter Mean -- Ruth Brown	--	Atlantic
47.	Secret Love -- Caterina Valente	--	Decca
48.	Philadelphia, USA -- The Nu Tornadoes	--	Carlton
49.	Donde Esta Santa Claus -- Augie Rios	[illegible]	Metro
50.	Rainbow Riot -- Bill Doggett		King

1. TULSA'S TOP REFRESHMENT TREAT . . . THIS WEEK . . . AND EVERY WEEK . . .

Pepsi-Cola

The first version of the KAKC Top 50 record survey was a legal-sized sheet, typed and mimeographed. This one, from December 8, 1958, shows that the No. 1 slot during that holiday season belonged to "The Chipmunk Song" by the Chipmunks, a Christmas classic (originally issued on red vinyl) that launched a franchise that has spanned the generations. Songs by the Platters, Elvis Presley, Ray Charles, and Sam Cooke are also in the Top 10. (Courtesy of Dick Schmitz.)

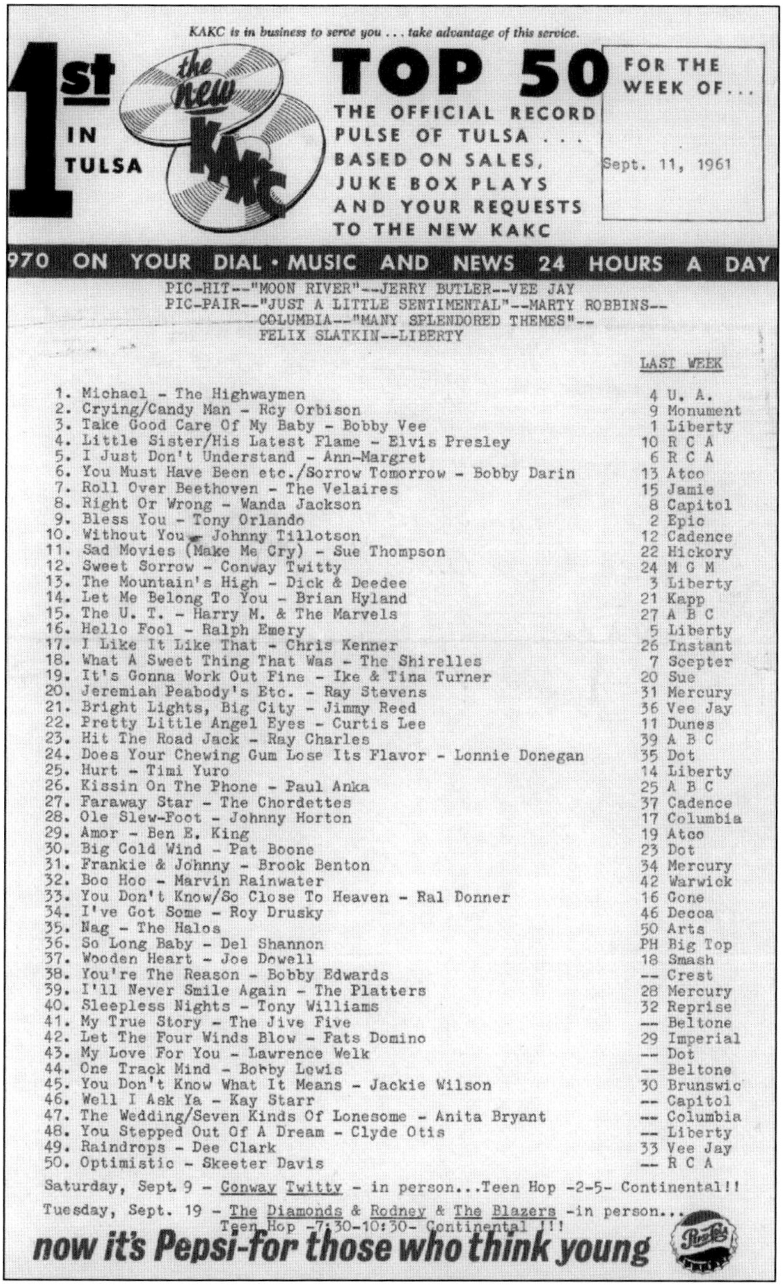

KAKC is in business to serve you . . . take advantage of this service.

1st IN TULSA — the new KAKC — TOP 50 THE OFFICIAL RECORD PULSE OF TULSA . . . BASED ON SALES, JUKE BOX PLAYS AND YOUR REQUESTS TO THE NEW KAKC

FOR THE WEEK OF... Sept. 11, 1961

970 ON YOUR DIAL • MUSIC AND NEWS 24 HOURS A DAY

PIC-HIT--"MOON RIVER"--JERRY BUTLER--VEE JAY
PIC-PAIR--"JUST A LITTLE SENTIMENTAL"--MARTY ROBBINS--COLUMBIA--"MANY SPLENDORED THEMES"--FELIX SLATKIN--LIBERTY

		LAST WEEK	
1.	Michael - The Highwaymen	4	U. A.
2.	Crying/Candy Man - Roy Orbison	9	Monument
3.	Take Good Care Of My Baby - Bobby Vee	1	Liberty
4.	Little Sister/His Latest Flame - Elvis Presley	10	R C A
5.	I Just Don't Understand - Ann-Margret	6	R C A
6.	You Must Have Been etc./Sorrow Tomorrow - Bobby Darin	13	Atco
7.	Roll Over Beethoven - The Velaires	15	Jamie
8.	Right Or Wrong - Wanda Jackson	8	Capitol
9.	Bless You - Tony Orlando	2	Epic
10.	Without You - Johnny Tillotson	12	Cadence
11.	Sad Movies (Make Me Cry) - Sue Thompson	22	Hickory
12.	Sweet Sorrow - Conway Twitty	24	M G M
13.	The Mountain's High - Dick & Deedee	3	Liberty
14.	Let Me Belong To You - Brian Hyland	21	Kapp
15.	The U. T. - Harry M. & The Marvels	27	A B C
16.	Hello Fool - Ralph Emery	5	Liberty
17.	I Like It Like That - Chris Kenner	26	Instant
18.	What A Sweet Thing That Was - The Shirelles	7	Scepter
19.	It's Gonna Work Out Fine - Ike & Tina Turner	20	Sue
20.	Jeremiah Peabody's Etc. - Ray Stevens	31	Mercury
21.	Bright Lights, Big City - Jimmy Reed	36	Vee Jay
22.	Pretty Little Angel Eyes - Curtis Lee	11	Dunes
23.	Hit The Road Jack - Ray Charles	39	A B C
24.	Does Your Chewing Gum Lose Its Flavor - Lonnie Donegan	35	Dot
25.	Hurt - Timi Yuro	14	Liberty
26.	Kissin On The Phone - Paul Anka	25	A B C
27.	Faraway Star - The Chordettes	37	Cadence
28.	Ole Slew-Foot - Johnny Horton	17	Columbia
29.	Amor - Ben E. King	19	Atco
30.	Big Cold Wind - Pat Boone	23	Dot
31.	Frankie & Johnny - Brook Benton	34	Mercury
32.	Boo Hoo - Marvin Rainwater	42	Warwick
33.	You Don't Know/So Close To Heaven - Ral Donner	16	Gone
34.	I've Got Some - Roy Drusky	46	Decca
35.	Nag - The Halos	50	Arts
36.	So Long Baby - Del Shannon	PH	Big Top
37.	Wooden Heart - Joe Dowell	18	Smash
38.	You're The Reason - Bobby Edwards	--	Crest
39.	I'll Never Smile Again - The Platters	28	Mercury
40.	Sleepless Nights - Tony Williams	32	Reprise
41.	My True Story - The Jive Five	--	Beltone
42.	Let The Four Winds Blow - Fats Domino	29	Imperial
43.	My Love For You - Lawrence Welk	--	Dot
44.	One Track Mind - Bobby Lewis	--	Beltone
45.	You Don't Know What It Means - Jackie Wilson	30	Brunswic
46.	Well I Ask Ya - Kay Starr	--	Capitol
47.	The Wedding/Seven Kinds Of Lonesome - Anita Bryant	--	Columbia
48.	You Stepped Out Of A Dream - Clyde Otis	--	Liberty
49.	Raindrops - Dee Clark	33	Vee Jay
50.	Optimistic - Skeeter Davis	--	R C A

Saturday, Sept. 9 - Conway Twitty - in person...Teen Hop -2-5- Continental!!
Tuesday, Sept. 19 - The Diamonds & Rodney & The Blazers -in person...Teen Hop -7:30-10:30- Continental !!!

An updated masthead adorned the second version of the legal-sized KAKC Top 50 survey. No. 1 on September 11, 1961, was a folk song, "Michael" (fully titled "Michael, Row Your Boat Ashore"), by the Highwaymen. Roy Orbison's classic "Crying" and Bobby Vee's "Take Good Care of My Baby" round out the top three. This chart shows the variety of musical styles that a Top 40 station played. Rock, folk, country, R&B, and easy listening are all represented. Lawrence Welk is even included, at No. 43. And, there were the novelty hits, like the No. 24 song on this list. Song No. 47 is by former Miss KAKC Anita Bryant, who finished second runner-up in the Miss America pageant in 1958. By this time, Bryant was a Columbia Records recording artist. (Courtesy of Wayne McCombs.)

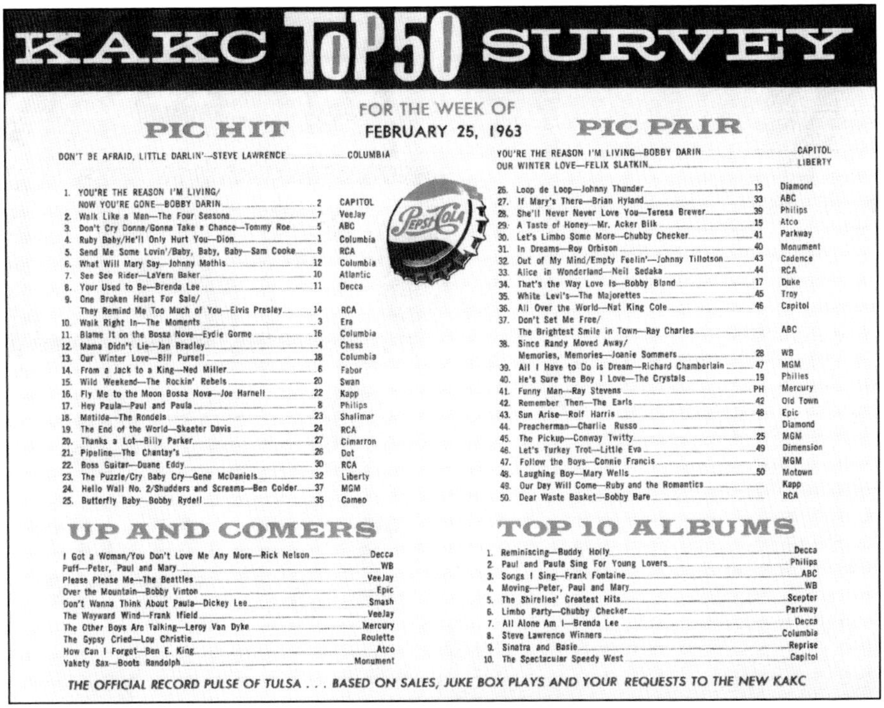

KAKC TOP 50 SURVEY

FOR THE WEEK OF FEBRUARY 25, 1963

PIC HIT

DON'T BE AFRAID, LITTLE DARLIN'—STEVE LAWRENCE .... COLUMBIA

PIC PAIR

YOU'RE THE REASON I'M LIVING—BOBBY DARIN .... CAPITOL
OUR WINTER LOVE—FELIX SLATKIN .... LIBERTY

No.	Title—Artist	Last Week	Label
1.	YOU'RE THE REASON I'M LIVING/ NOW YOU'RE GONE—BOBBY DARIN	2	CAPITOL
2.	Walk Like a Man—The Four Seasons	7	VeeJay
3.	Don't Cry Donna/Gonna Take a Chance—Tommy Roe	5	ABC
4.	Ruby Baby/He'll Only Hurt You—Dion	1	Columbia
5.	Send Me Some Lovin'/Baby, Baby, Baby—Sam Cooke	9	RCA
6.	What Will Mary Say—Johnny Mathis	12	Columbia
7.	See See Rider—LaVern Baker	10	Atlantic
8.	Your Used to Be—Brenda Lee	11	Decca
9.	One Broken Heart For Sale/ They Remind Me Too Much of You—Elvis Presley	14	RCA
10.	Walk Right In—The Moments	3	Era
11.	Blame It on the Bossa Nova—Eydie Gorme	16	Columbia
12.	Mama Didn't Lie—Jan Bradley	4	Chess
13.	Our Winter Love—Bill Pursell	18	Columbia
14.	From a Jack to a King—Ned Miller	6	Fabor
15.	Wild Weekend—The Rockin' Rebels	20	Swan
16.	Fly Me to the Moon Bossa Nova—Joe Harnell	22	Kapp
17.	Hey Paula—Paul and Paula	8	Philips
18.	Matilda—The Rondels	23	Shalimar
19.	The End of the World—Skeeter Davis	24	RCA
20.	Thanks a Lot—Billy Parker	27	Cimarron
21.	Pipeline—The Chantay's	26	Dot
22.	Boss Guitar—Duane Eddy	30	RCA
23.	The Puzzle/Cry Baby Cry—Gene McDaniels	32	Liberty
24.	Hello Wall No. 2/Shudders and Screams—Ben Colder	37	MGM
25.	Butterfly Baby—Bobby Rydell	35	Cameo
26.	Loop de Loop—Johnny Thunder	13	Diamond
27.	If Mary's There—Brian Hyland	33	ABC
28.	She'll Never Never Love You—Teresa Brewer	39	Philips
29.	A Taste of Honey—Mr. Acker Bilk	15	Atco
30.	Let's Limbo Some More—Chubby Checker	41	Parkway
31.	In Dreams—Roy Orbison	40	Monument
32.	Out of My Mind/Empty Feelin'—Johnny Tillotson	43	Cadence
33.	Alice in Wonderland—Neil Sedaka	44	RCA
34.	That's the Way Love Is—Bobby Bland	17	Duke
35.	White Levi's—The Majorettes	45	Troy
36.	All Over the World—Nat King Cole	46	Capitol
37.	Don't Set Me Free/ The Brightest Smile in Town—Ray Charles		ABC
38.	Since Randy Moved Away/ Memories, Memories—Joanie Sommers	28	WB
39.	All I Have to Do is Dream—Richard Chamberlain	47	MGM
40.	He's Sure the Boy I Love—The Crystals	19	Philles
41.	Funny Man—Ray Stevens	PH	Mercury
42.	Remember Then—The Earls	42	Old Town
43.	Sun Arise—Rolf Harris	48	Epic
44.	Preacherman—Charlie Russo		Diamond
45.	The Pickup—Conway Twitty	25	MGM
46.	Let's Turkey Trot—Little Eva	49	Dimension
47.	Follow the Boys—Connie Francis		MGM
48.	Laughing Boy—Mary Wells	50	Motown
49.	Our Day Will Come—Ruby and the Romantics		Kapp
50.	Dear Waste Basket—Bobby Bare		RCA

UP AND COMERS

I Got a Woman/You Don't Love Me Any More—Rick Nelson	Decca
Puff—Peter, Paul and Mary	WB
Please Please Me—The Beattles	VeeJay
Over the Mountain—Bobby Vinton	Epic
Don't Wanna Think About Paula—Dickey Lee	Smash
The Wayward Wind—Frank Ifield	VeeJay
The Other Boys Are Talking—Leroy Van Dyke	Mercury
The Gypsy Cried—Lou Christie	Roulette
How Can I Forget—Ben E. King	Atco
Yakety Sax—Boots Randolph	Monument

TOP 10 ALBUMS

1.	Reminiscing—Buddy Holly	Decca
2.	Paul and Paula Sing For Young Lovers	Philips
3.	Songs I Sing—Frank Fontaine	ABC
4.	Moving—Peter, Paul and Mary	WB
5.	The Shirelles' Greatest Hits	Scepter
6.	Limbo Party—Chubby Checker	Parkway
7.	All Alone Am I—Brenda Lee	Decca
8.	Steve Lawrence Winners	Columbia
9.	Sinatra and Basie	Reprise
10.	The Spectacular Speedy West	Capitol

THE OFFICIAL RECORD PULSE OF TULSA . . . BASED ON SALES, JUKE BOX PLAYS AND YOUR REQUESTS TO THE NEW KAKC

The longest-running (1962–1967) version of the KAKC Top 50 was a foldable sheet that featured photographs of the Big 7 deejays. The February 25, 1963, survey above features songs by Bobby Darin, the Four Seasons, Dion, and Sam Cooke. The surveys are great for tracking the constantly changing lineup of the Big 7 deejays. Don Kelly (and his sidekick, Chauncey), Roger Rocka, and Tom York would all depart the station later that year. (Both, courtesy of Wayne McCombs.)

KAKC TOP 50 SURVEY

MARCH 23, 1964

PIC HIT

TODAY – THE NEW CHRISTY MINSTRELS .... COLUMBIA

PIC PAIR

KISSIN' COUSINS – ELVIS PRESLEY (SOUNDTRACK) .... RCA
HOT ROD DANCE PARTY–JERRY COLE AND HIS SPACEMEN .. CAPITOL

1. TWIST AND SHOUT – THE BEATLES .... 1 TOLLIE
2. Kissin' Cousins/It Hurts Me – Elvis Presley .... 3 RCA
3. Please Please Me/From Me to You – The Beatles .... 2 Vee Jay
4. Fun, Fun, Fun – The Beach Boys .... 7 Capitol
5. California Sun – The Rivieras .... 4 Riviera
6. My Heart Belongs to Only You – Bobby Vinton .... 10 Epic
7. Hi-Heel Sneakers – Tommy Tucker .... 13 Checker
8. She Loves You – The Beatles .... 5 Swan
9. Hey Jean, Hey Dean – Dean and Jean .... 11 Rust
10. Who Do You Love – The Sapphires .... 19 Swan
11. Lonely Avenue – The Crickets .... 9 Liberty
12. Gonna Send You Back to Georgia – Timmy Shaw .... 15 Wand
13. Dead Man's Curve/
The New Girl in School – Jan and Dean .... 23 Liberty
14. Dawn (Go Away) – The Four Seasons .... 6 Philips
15. Lonnie on the Move – Lonnie Mack .... 17 Fraternity
16. Java – Al Hirt .... 8 RCA
17. Penetration – The Pyramids .... 24 Best
18. Heartbreak Ahead – The Murmaids .... 21 Chattahoochee
19. Can't Buy Me Love/You Can't Do That – The Beatles .... 35 Capitol
20. Nadine – Chuck Berry .... 30 Chess
21. Tell It on the Mountain – Peter, Paul and Mary .... 25 WB
22. Abigail Beecher – Freddy Cannon .... 12 WB
23. The Shelter of Your Arms – Sammy Davis Junior .... 27 Reprise
24. Can Your Monkey Do the Dog – Rufus Thomas .... 28 Stax
25. Convicted – The Dartells .... 29 Dot
26. Think/The Waiting Game – Brenda Lee .... 33 Decca
27. Navy Blue – Diane Renay 14 20th
28. Jailer, Bring Me Water – Trini Lopez .... 31 Reprise
29. Baby, Don't You Cry/
My Heart Cries for You – Ray Charles .... 34 ABC
30. We Love You, Beatles – The Carefrees .... 40 London
31. Ain't Gonna Tell Nobody – Jimmy Gilmer .... 36 Dot
32. I Want to Hold Your Hand/
I Saw Her Standing There – The Beatles .... 16 Capitol
33. Glad All Over – The Dave Clark Five .... 45 Epic
34. Stardust – April Stevens and Nino Tempo .... 38 Atco
35. Blue Winter/
You Know You Don't Want Me – Connie Francis .... 18 MGM
36. Hello, Dolly! – Louie Armstrong .... 39 Kapp
37. Suspicion – Terry Stafford .... 47 Crusader
38. Money – The Kingsmen .... 42 Wand
39. White on White – Danny Williams .... 43 UA
40. Good News – Sam Cooke .... 20 RCA
41. Hippy Hippy Shake – The Swinging Blue Jeans .... 46 Imperial
42. Break-A-Way – Irma Thomas .... 44 Imperial
43. Forever – Pete Drake .... 49 Smash
44. Spread Joy/Hey Bobba Needle – Chubby Checker .... 50 Parkway
45. That's the Way Boys Are – Lesley Gore .... PH Mercury
46. Shangri-La – Robert Maxwell .... Decca
47. Puppy Love – Barbara Lewis .... 22 Atlantic
48. Needles and Pins – The Searchers .... Kapp
49. Thank You, Girl/
Do You Want to Know a Secret – The Beatles .... Vee Jay
50. The Way You Do the Things You Do – The Temptations .. 51 Gordy

UP AND COMERS

The World I Used to Know – Jimmie Rodgers .... Dot
Charade – Sammy Kaye Orchestra .... Decca
Book of Love – The Raindrops .... Jubilee
A Girl Never Knows – Connie Stevens .... WB
Pink Panther – Plas. Johnson .... Capitol
Kiss Me, Sailor – Diane Renay 20th
The Matador – Major Lance .... Okeh
Our Faded Love – The Royaltones .... Mala
My Guy – Mary Wells .... Motown
Mexican Drummer Man – Herb Alpert's Tijuana Brass .... A&M

FIFTY-ONE'RS

The Beatles E.P. .... Vee Jay
You Lied to Your Daddy – The Tams .... ABC
Roll Over, Beethoven – The Beatles .... Capitol
Don't Let the Rains Come Down – The Serendipity Singers .... Philips
Ebb Tide – Lenny Welch .... Cadence
I Wish You Love – Gloria Lynne .... Everest
Little Beatle Boy – The Angels .... Smash
Susie – Jim Wolfe and the T-Towners .... T-Town
Meet the Beatles L.P. .... Capitol
...and nothing by The Bugs .... ? ? ?

THE OFFICIAL RECORD PULSE OF TULSA . . . BASED ON SALES, JUKE BOX PLAYS AND YOUR REQUESTS TO THE NEW KAKC

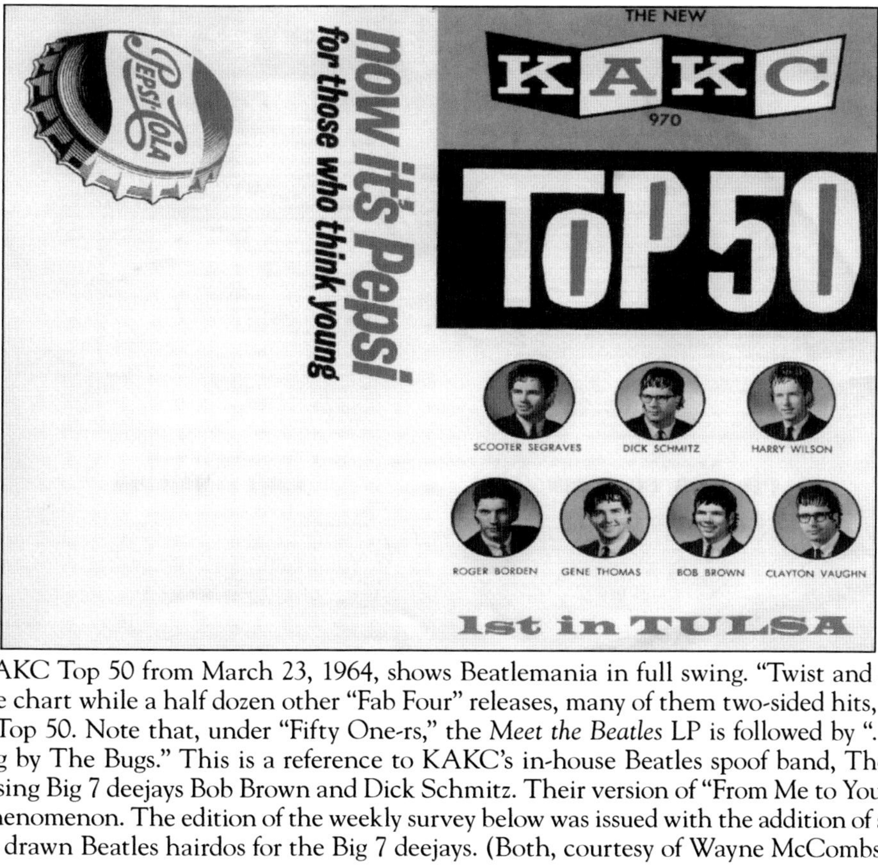

The KAKC Top 50 from March 23, 1964, shows Beatlemania in full swing. "Twist and Shout" tops the chart while a half dozen other "Fab Four" releases, many of them two-sided hits, appear in the Top 50. Note that, under "Fifty One-rs," the *Meet the Beatles* LP is followed by ". . . and nothing by The Bugs." This is a reference to KAKC's in-house Beatles spoof band, The Bugs, comprising Big 7 deejays Bob Brown and Dick Schmitz. Their version of "From Me to You" was a local phenomenon. The edition of the weekly survey below was issued with the addition of special, crudely drawn Beatles hairdos for the Big 7 deejays. (Both, courtesy of Wayne McCombs.)

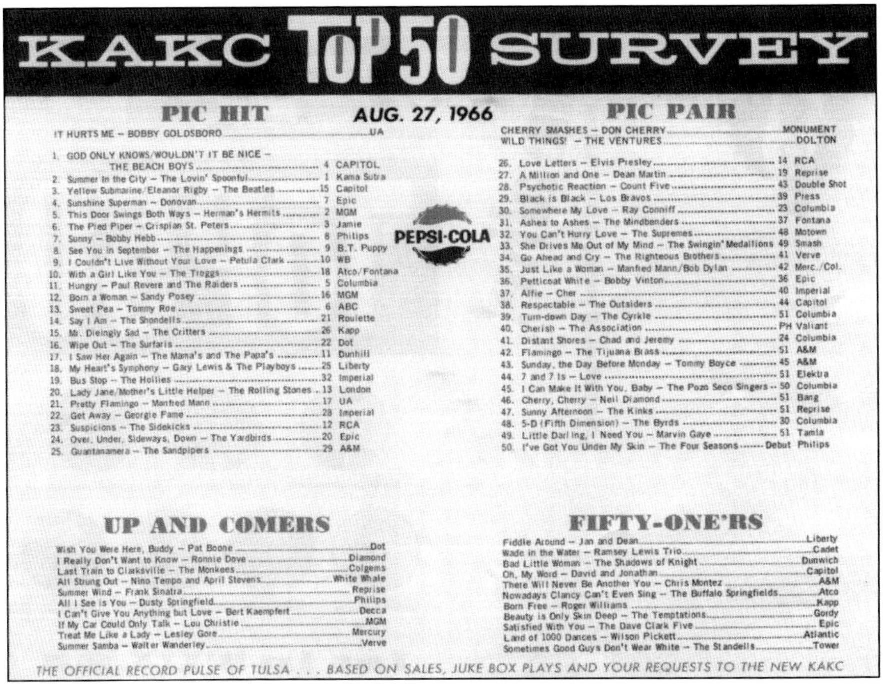

KAKC TOP 50 SURVEY

AUG. 27, 1966

PIC HIT

IT HURTS ME – BOBBY GOLDSBORO .... UA

#	Title – Artist	Last	Label
1.	GOD ONLY KNOWS/WOULDN'T IT BE NICE – THE BEACH BOYS	4	CAPITOL
2.	Summer In the City – The Lovin' Spoonful	1	Kama Sutra
3.	Yellow Submarine/Eleanor Rigby – The Beatles	15	Capitol
4.	Sunshine Superman – Donovan	7	Epic
5.	This Door Swings Both Ways – Herman's Hermits	2	MGM
6.	The Pied Piper – Crispian St. Peters	3	Jamie
7.	Sunny – Bobby Hebb	8	Philips
8.	See You in September – The Happenings	9	B.T. Puppy
9.	I Couldn't Live Without Your Love – Petula Clark	10	WB
10.	With a Girl Like You – The Troggs	18	Atco/Fontana
11.	Hungry – Paul Revere and The Raiders	5	Columbia
12.	Born a Woman – Sandy Posey	16	MGM
13.	Sweet Pea – Tommy Roe	6	ABC
14.	Say I Am – The Shondells	21	Roulette
15.	Mr. Dieingly Sad – The Critters	26	Kapp
16.	Wipe Out – The Surfaris	22	Dot
17.	I Saw Her Again – The Mama's and The Papa's	11	Dunhill
18.	My Heart's Symphony – Gary Lewis & The Playboys	25	Liberty
19.	Bus Stop – The Hollies	32	Imperial
20.	Lady Jane/Mother's Little Helper – The Rolling Stones	13	London
21.	Pretty Flamingo – Manfred Mann	17	UA
22.	Get Away – Georgie Fame	28	Imperial
23.	Suspicions – The Sidekicks	12	RCA
24.	Over, Under, Sideways, Down – The Yardbirds	20	Epic
25.	Guantanamera – The Sandpipers	29	A&M

PIC PAIR

CHERRY SMASHES – DON CHERRY .... MONUMENT
WILD THINGS! – THE VENTURES .... DOLTON

#	Title – Artist	Last	Label
26.	Love Letters – Elvis Presley	14	RCA
27.	A Million and One – Dean Martin	19	Reprise
28.	Psychotic Reaction – Count Five	43	Double Shot
29.	Black is Black – Los Bravos	39	Press
30.	Somewhere My Love – Ray Conniff	23	Columbia
31.	Ashes to Ashes – The Mindbenders	37	Fontana
32.	You Can't Hurry Love – The Supremes	48	Motown
33.	She Drives Me Out of My Mind – The Swingin' Medallions	49	Smash
34.	Go Ahead and Cry – The Righteous Brothers	41	Verve
35.	Just Like a Woman – Manfred Mann/Bob Dylan	42	Merc./Col.
36.	Petticoat White – Bobby Vinton	36	Epic
37.	Alfie – Cher	40	Imperial
38.	Respectable – The Outsiders	44	Capitol
39.	Turn-down Day – The Cyrkle	51	Columbia
40.	Cherish – The Association	PH	Valiant
41.	Distant Shores – Chad and Jeremy	24	Columbia
42.	Flamingo – The Tijuana Brass	51	A&M
43.	Sunday, the Day Before Monday – Tommy Boyce	45	A&M
44.	7 and 7 Is – Love	51	Elektra
45.	I Can Make It With You, Baby – The Pozo Seco Singers	50	Columbia
46.	Cherry, Cherry – Neil Diamond	51	Bang
47.	Sunny Afternoon – The Kinks	51	Reprise
48.	5-D (Fifth Dimension) – The Byrds	30	Columbia
49.	Little Darling, I Need You – Marvin Gaye	51	Tamla
50.	I've Got You Under My Skin – The Four Seasons	Debut	Philips

UP AND COMERS

Wish You Were Here, Buddy – Pat Boone	Dot
I Really Don't Want to Know – Ronnie Dove	Diamond
Last Train to Clarksville – The Monkees	Colgems
All Strung Out – Nino Tempo and April Stevens	White Whale
Summer Wind – Frank Sinatra	Reprise
All I See is You – Dusty Springfield	Philips
I Can't Give You Anything but Love – Bert Kaempfert	Decca
If My Car Could Only Talk – Lou Christie	MGM
Treat Me Like a Lady – Lesley Gore	Mercury
Summer Samba – Walter Wanderley	Verve

FIFTY-ONE'RS

Fiddle Around – Jan and Dean	Liberty
Wade in the Water – Ramsey Lewis Trio	Cadet
Bad Little Woman – The Shadows of Knight	Dunwich
Oh, My Word – David and Jonathan	Capitol
There Will Never Be Another You – Chris Montez	A&M
Nowadays Clancy Can't Even Sing – The Buffalo Springfields	Atco
Born Free – Roger Williams	Kapp
Beauty is Only Skin Deep – The Temptations	Gordy
Satisfied With You – The Dave Clark Five	Epic
Land of 1000 Dances – Wilson Pickett	Atlantic
Sometimes Good Guys Don't Wear White – The Standells	Tower

THE OFFICIAL RECORD PULSE OF TULSA . . . BASED ON SALES, JUKE BOX PLAYS AND YOUR REQUESTS TO THE NEW KAKC

This Top 50 survey from August 27, 1966, shows the Beach Boys at No. 1 with the double-sized smash God Only Knows/Wouldn't It Be Nice. In 1966, the US charts contained many songs by British artists, including the Beatles, Herman's Hermits, Donovan, the Troggs, the Hollies, Yardbirds, and Petula Clark. Below, the Big 7 deejays lineup has experienced nearly a complete turnover in three years. Only Scooter Segraves remains from the 1963 survey featured in this chapter. The newest members of the Big 7 are Jim Wight and Jerry Clark. Note the new Pepsi slogan, perhaps their best of that era: "Come Alive! You're in the Pepsi generation!" (Both, courtesy of Wayne McCombs.)

KAKC'S "BIG 30" RECORDS IN GREATER TULSA

ISSUE NO. 31—SEPTEMBER 20, 1967

LAST WEEK	THIS WEEK	TITLE	ARTIST	LABEL	WEEKS ON BIG 30
1	1	THE LETTER	The Box Tops	Mala	6
4	2	I HAD A DREAM	Paul Revere & The Raiders	Columbia	5
2	3	REFLECTIONS	Diana Ross & The Supremes	Motown	7
10	4	LITTLE OLE MAN	Bill Cosby	Warner Bros.	3
6	5	TWELVE-THIRTY	The Mamas & The Papas	Dunhill	6
13	6	NEVER, MY LOVE	The Association	Warner Bros.	4
8	7	IT'S THE LITTLE THINGS	Sonny & Cher	Atco	8
9	8	GETTIN' TOGETHER	Tommy James & The Shondells	Roulette	6
18	9	BROWN-EYED GIRL	Van Morrison	Bang	4
15	10	YOU KNOW WHAT I MEAN	The Turtles	White Whale	7
5	11	THERE IS A MOUNTAIN	Donovan	Epic	7
19	12	APPLES, PEACHES, PUMPKIN PIE	Jay & The Techniques	Smash	5
17	13	THE CAT IN THE WINDOW	Petula Clark	Warner Bros.	5
16	14	GIMME LITTLE SIGN	Brenton Wood	Double Shot	5
3	15	ODE TO BILLIE JOE	Bobbie Gentry	Capitol	9
7	16	SOUL FINGER	The Bar-Kays	Volt	8
23	17	THE LOOK OF LOVE	Dusty Springfield	Philips	4
22	18	WHAT NOW, MY LOVE	Mitch Ryder	DynoVoice	3
25	19	HEY BABY, THEY'RE PLAYING OUR SONG	The Buckinghams	Columbia	2
14	20	I DIG ROCK AND ROLL MUSIC	Peter, Paul & Mary	Warner Bros.	6
24	21	I MAKE A FOOL OF MYSELF	Frankie Valli	Philips	4
11	22	WORDS	The Monkees	Colgems	12
28	23	HOW CAN I BE SURE	The Young Rascals	Atlantic	2
27	24	LOVE STORY	The Brothers	White Whale	3
26	25	HIGHER AND HIGHER	Jackie Wilson	Brunswick	2
HB	26	HOLIDAY	The Bee Gees	Atco	1
29	27	GROOVIN'	Booker T & The MGs	Stax	2
30	28	LET LOVE COME BETWEEN US	James & Bobby Purify	Bell	1
HB	29	WE LOVE YOU	The Rolling Stones	London	1
HB	30	GO WITH ME	Gene & Debbe	TRX	1

THE POPULARITY OF RECORDS LISTED HEREIN IS THE OPINION OF KAKC, BASED ON ITS SURVEY OF RECORD SALES IN TULSA CORRELATED WITH LISTENER REQUESTS.

With consultant Bill Drake's involvement in 1967 came the new *Big 30* survey. It featured a different deejay photograph or graphic each week. On September 20, 1967, "The Letter" by the Box Tops is No. 1. The 1968 *Big 30* below promotes the Million Dollar Battle, in which the top "heavyweights" of all time were pitted against each other. A song (like "Light My Fire," depicted in the graphic) would be played, and then a challenger (such as "Cherish") was introduced and played. Listeners would call during the song and vote for the one they liked best. KAKC would then play the winning song again, followed by another challenger. (Both, courtesy of Wayne McCombs.)

KAKC THE BIG 97

PRESENTS THE BIG 30

ISSUE NO. 140 — NOVEMBER 12, 1969

This Week	Last Week	Title / Artist/Label	Weeks on Big 30
1	2	SUITE: JUDY BLUE EYES *Crosby, Stills, and Nash — Atlantic*	5
2	1	NA NA HEY HEY KISS HIM GOODBYE *Steam — Fontana*	6
3	6	GOING IN CIRCLES *The Friends of Distinction — RCA*	4
4	10	FORTUNATE SON/DOWN ON THE CORNER *Creedence Clearwater Revival — Fantasy*	4
5	7	YOU'VE LOST THAT LOVIN' FEELING *Dionne Warwick — Scepter*	5
6	8	AND WHEN I DIE *Blood, Sweat and Tears — Columbia*	4
7	5	WEDDING BELL BLUES *The 5th Dimension — Soul City*	8
8	9	TRY A LITTLE KINDNESS *Glen Campbell — Capitol*	6
9	3	SOMETHING *The Beatles — Apple*	6
10	13	ROOSEVELT AND IRE LEE *Tony Joe White — Monument*	4
11	12	BALL OF FIRE *Tommy James and The Shondells — Roulette*	6
12	16	EARLY IN THE MORNING *Vanity Fare — Page One*	5
13	4	UNDUN *The Guess Who — RCA*	7
14	19	SOMEDAY WE'LL BE TOGETHER *Diana Ross and The Supremes — Motown*	3
15	11	ONE TIN SOLDIER *The Original Caste — T·A*	8
16	21	YESTER-ME, YESTER-YOU, YESTERDAY *Stevie Wonder — Tamla*	3
17	27	TAKE A LETTER MARIA *R. B. Greaves — Atco*	2
18	22	LADY JANE *The Plastic Cow Goes Moooooog — Dot*	3
19	15	SO GOOD TOGETHER *Andy Kim — Steed*	7
20	26	LEAVING ON A JET PLANE *Peter, Paul and Mary — W7*	3
21	24	SHANGRI-LA *The Lettermen — Capitol*	5
22	30	CHERRY HILL PARK *Billy Joe Royal — Columbia*	2
23	18	THE COLOUR OF MY LOVE *Jefferson — Decca*	7
24	29	HOLLY HOLY *Neil Diamond — Uni*	2
25	28	BABY, I'M FOR REAL *The Originals — Soul*	2
26	HB	CUPID *Johnny Nash — Jad*	1
27	HB	ELI'S COMING *Three Dog Night — Dunbill*	1
28	HB	SHE BELONGS TO ME *Rick Nelson — Decca*	1
29	HB	HEAVEN KNOWS *The Grass Roots — Dunhill*	1
30	HB	BRINGING ON BACK THE GOOD TIMES *The Love Affair — Date*	1

The listing of records herein is the opinion of KAKC, based on its survey of retail sales, listener requests, and KAKC's judgment of each records appeal.

HITBOUNDS

RAINDROPS KEEP FALLIN' ON MY HEAD — B. J. Thomas (Scepter)

SHE'S READY — Spiral Staircase (Columbia)

BACKFIELD IN MOTION — Mel and Tim (Bamboo)

KAKC THE BIG 97

PRESENTS THE BIG 30

ISSUE NO. 197 — DECEMBER 16, 1970

This Week	Last Week	Title / Artist/Label	Weeks on Big 30
1	8	KNOCK THREE TIMES *Dawn — Bell*	4
2	1	MY SWEET LORD *George Harrison — Apple*	5
3	2	I THINK I LOVE YOU *Partridge Family — Bell*	6
4	5	FEEL ALLRIGHT *Cargoe — Beautiful*	6
5	4	ONE MAN BAND *3 Dog Night — Dunhill*	7
6	11	STONED LOVE *Supremes — Motown*	7
7	3	IMMIGRANT SONG *Led Zeppelin — Atlantic*	6
8	15	WHO NEEDS YA *Steppenwolf — Dunbill*	3
9	21	ONE LESS BELL TO ANSWER *5th Dimension — Bell*	3
10	6	DOES ANYBODY REALLY KNOW WHAT TIME IT IS *Chicago — Columbia*	7
11	13	BE MY BABY *Andy Kim — Steed*	6
12	22	MOST OF ALL *B.J. Thomas — Scepter*	3
13	7	GAMES *Redeye — Pentagram*	8
14	9	GYPSY WOMAN *Brian Hyland — Uni*	9
15	16	YOU BETTER THINK TWICE *Poco — Epic*	6
16	18	SO CLOSE *Jake Holmes — Polydor*	5
17	26	HOME SWEET OKLAHOMA *Leon Russell & The Shelter People—Shelter*	2
18	19	5-10-15-20 (25-30 YEARS OF LOVE) *The Presidents — Sussex*	5
19	29	YOUR SONG *Elton John — Uni*	2
20	20	NO MATTER WHAT *Badfinger — Apple*	5
21	10	MONTEGO BAY *Bobby Bloom — MGM*	8
22	27	LOVE THE ONE YOU'RE WITH *Stephen Stills — Atco*	3
23	25	SILVER MOON *Michael Nesmith & The First National Band — RCA*	4
24	30	STONEY END *Barbra Streisand — Columbia*	2
25	28	RIVER DEEP - MOUNTAIN HIGH *Supremes/4 Tops — Motown*	2
26	HB	WE GOTTA GET YOU A WOMAN *Runt — Ampex*	1
27	HB	RIGHT ON *Rascals — Atlantic*	1
28	HB	FOR THE GOOD TIMES *Ray Price — Columbia*	1
29	HB	BORN TO WANDER *Rare Earth — Rare Earth*	1
30	HB	THEY CAN'T TAKE AWAY OUR MUSIC *Eric Burdon & War — MGM*	1

The listing of records herein is the opinion of KAKC, based on its survey of retail sales, listener requests, and KAKC's judgment of each records appeal.

HITBOUNDS

HOLLY HOLY — Jr. Walker & The All Stars (Soul)

LET THE WATER RUN DOWN — Vin Cardinal (A&M)

THE SHAPE I'M IN — The Band (Capitol)

In 1968, KAKC introduced a new version of the *Big 30*, which unfolded to reveal a long, skinny list of songs. On the survey to the left, from November 12, 1969, "Suite: Judy Blue Eyes" by Crosby, Stills & Nash is No. 1. As the 1960s draw to a close, two of the decade's icons release their final hits—Diana Ross & the Supremes with "Someday We'll Be Together" and Peter, Paul and Mary with "Leaving on a Jet Plane" (written by John Denver). This survey is also notable for containing three compositions by one of the top songwriters of the era. "And When I Die," "Wedding Bell Blues" and "Eli's Coming" were all penned by Laura Nyro. To the right, local artists rule on this *Big 30* from December 14, 1970. Tulsa band Cargoe has "Feel Alright" [*sic*], a song produced by KAKC's Robert W. Walker, at No. 4. Leon Russell's "Home Sweet Oklahoma" ranks at No. 17. (Courtesy of Wayne McCombs.)

THE BIG 97 HITS OF 1967
as compiled by 97'KAKC

1. LIGHT MY FIRE — The Doors
2. WINDY — The Association
3. WORDS — The Monkees
4. KIND OF A DRAG — The Buckinghams
5. PENNY LANE — The Beatles
6. ON A CAROUSEL — The Hollies
7. MY CUP RUNNETH OVER — Ed Ames
8. COME BACK WHEN YOU GROW UP — Bobby Vee
9. HAPPY TOGETHER — The Turtles
10. ODE TO BILLY JOE — Bobbie Gentry
11. DO IT AGAIN A LITTLE BIT SLOWER — Jon and Robin
12. GEORGY GIRL — The Seekers
13. THE LETTER — The Box Tops
14. SOCIETY'S CHILD — Janis Ian
15. CAN'T TAKE MY EYES OFF YOU — Frankie Valli
16. INCENSE AND PEPPERMINTS — Strawberry Alarm Clock
17. FOR WHAT IT'S WORTH — Buffalo Springfield
18. NO MILK TODAY — Herman's Hermits
19. NEVER, MY LOVE — The Association
20. THE RAIN, THE PARK, AND OTHER THINGS — The Cowsills
21. SUMMER WINE — Nancy and Lee
22. RESPECT — Aretha Franklin
23. GROOVIN' — The Young Rascals
24. ALL YOU NEED IS LOVE — The Beatles
25. SILENCE IS GOLDEN — The Tremeloes
26. DAYDREAM BELIEVER — The Monkees
27. THE HAPPENING — The Supremes
28. TO SIR WITH LOVE — Lulu
29. WESTERN UNION — The 5 Americans
30. HOLIDAY — The Bee Gees
31. I THINK WE'RE ALONE NOW — Tommy James
32. REFLECTIONS — The Supremes
33. LITTLE OLE MAN — Bill Cosby
34. THE 59TH STREET BRIDGE SONG — Harper's Bizarre
35. A LITTLE BIT ME, A LITTLE BIT YOU — The Monkees
36. I WAS MADE TO LOVE HER — Stevie Wonder
37. COME ON DOWN TO MY BOAT — Every Mother's Son
38. SHE'D RATHER BE WITH ME — The Turtles
39. IT'S THE LITTLE THINGS — Sonny and Cher
40. I SAY A LITTLE PRAYER — Dionne Warwick
41. BEND ME, SHAPE ME — The American Breed
42. SOMETHING STUPID — Frank and Nancy Sinatra
43. A LITTLE BIT OF SOUL — Music Explosion
44. THE BEAT GOES ON — Sonny and Cher
45. THEN YOU CAN TELL ME GOODBYE — The Casinos
46. SOUL FINGER — The BarKays
47. LET IT OUT — The Hombres
48. THE TRACKS OF MY TEARS — Johnny Rivers
49. SOCK IT TO ME, BABY — Mitch Ryder
50. WHEN I WAS YOUNG — The Animals
51. TELL IT LIKE IT IS — Aaron Neville
52. CARRIE ANNE — The Hollies
53. BROWN EYED GIRL — Van Morrison
54. UPS AND DOWNS — Revere's Raiders
55. APPLES, PEACHES, PUMPKIN PIE — J and The Techniques
56. IN AND OUT OF LOVE — The Supremes
57. THIS IS MY SONG — Pet Clark
58. WHITE RABBIT — The Jefferson Airplane
59. JIMMY MACK — Martha and The Vandellas
60. JUDY IN DISGUISE — John Fred & Playboys
61. BABY, I NEED YOUR LOVING — Johnny Rivers
62. THE SOUND OF LOVE — The 5 Americans
63. THE LOOK OF LOVE — Dusty Springfield
64. DING DONG, THE WITCH IS DEAD — The Fifth Estate
65. HAPPY JACK — The Who
66. BLUE'S THEME — Davie Allen and Arrows
67. YOU KNOW WHAT I MEAN — The Turtles
68. THANK THE LORD FOR THE NIGHT TIME — Neil Diamond
69. GIMME SOME LOVIN' — The Spencer Davis Group
70. I CAN SEE FOR MILES — The Who
71. DON'T SLEEP IN THE SUBWAY — Pet Clark
72. MERCY, MERCY, MERCY — The Buckinghams
73. 98.6 — Keith
74. KEEP THE BALL ROLLING — J and The Techniques
75. RETURN OF THE RED BARON — The Royal Guardsmen
76. WALK TALL — Two of Clubs
77. PAPER CUP — The 5th Dimension
78. HELLO-GOODBYE — The Beatles
79. GIMME LITTLE SIGN — Brenton Wood
80. HEROES AND VILLAINS — The Beach Boys
81. CASINO ROYALE — Herb Alpert & the TJB
82. A WHITER SHADE OF PALE — Procol Harum
83. BY THE TIME I GET TO PHOENIX — Glen Campbell
84. STEP OUT OF YOUR MIND — The American Breed
85. BEAUTIFUL PEOPLE — Bobby Vee
86. EVERLASTING LOVE — Robert Knight
87. SWEET SOUL MUSIC — Arthur Conley
88. IT MUST BE HIM — Vikki Carr
89. SOMEBODY TO LOVE — Jefferson Airplane
90. WE AIN'T GOT NOTHING YET — The Blues Magoos
91. YOU'VE GOT WHAT IT TAKES — The Dave Clark 5
92. MUSTANG SALLY — Wilson Pickett
93. SUNSHINE GIRL — The Parade
94. BOWLING GREEN — The Everly Brothers
95. UP, UP, AND AWAY — The 5th Dimension
96. MUSIC TO WATCH GIRLS BY — The Bob Crew Generation
97. SHOW ME — Joe Tex

For many years, around the New Year's holiday, KAKC counted down the Big 97 songs of the entire year. Listeners enjoyed listening to see where their favorites came in and could write in for their own copy of the year-end rankings, which is how Tulsan Clyde Cole III acquired this 1967 list documenting a year that featured a lot of great music. (Courtesy of Clyde Cole III.)

TULSA'S TOP 100 OF THE 60's
97/KAKC

1.	LIGHT MY FIRE	THE DOORS	1967
2.	HEY JUDE	THE BEATLES	1968
3.	AQUARIUS/LET THE SUNSHINE IN	THE 5TH DIMENSION	1969
4.	THEME FROM A SUMMER PLACE	PERCY FAITH	1960
5.	CHERISH	THE ASSOCIATION	1966
6.	SATISFACTION	THE ROLLING STONES	1965
7.	LOUIE, LOUIE	THE KINGSMEN	1963
8.	THE HOUSE OF THE RISING SUN	THE ANIMALS	1964
9.	CALIFORNIA DREAMING	MAMAS & PAPAS	1966
10.	LOVE IS BLUE	PAUL MAURIAT	1968
11.	GET BACK	THE BEATLES	1969
12.	PRETTY WOMAN	ROY ORBISON	1964
13.	KICKS	PAUL REVERE/RAIDERS	1966
14.	MRS. ROBINSON	SIMON & GARFUNKLE	1968
15.	WINDY	THE ASSOCIATION	1967
16.	I WANT TO HOLD YOUR HAND	THE BEATLES	1964
17.	I CAN'T GET NEXT TO YOU	THE TEMPTATIONS	1969
18.	THE STRIPPER	DAVID ROSE	1962
19.	THESE BOOTS ARE MADE FOR WALKIN'	NANCY SINATRA	1966
20.	MRS. BROWN, YOU'VE GOT A LOVELY DAUGHTER	HERMAN'S HERMITS	1965
21.	GOOD VIBRATIONS	THE BEACH BOYS	1966
22.	BLUE VELVET	BOBBY VINTON	1963
23.	LAST TRAIN TO CLARKSVILLE	THE MONKEES	1966
24.	THE TWIST	CHUBBY CHECKER	1962
25.	SUGAR, SUGAR	THE ARCHIES	1969
26.	SAVE THE LAST DANCE FOR ME	THE DRIFTERS	1960
27.	HONKEY TONK WOMEN	THE ROLLING STONES	1969
28.	YOUNG GIRL	GARY PUCKETT/UNION GAP	1968
29.	KIND OF A DRAG	THE BUCKINGHAMS	1967
30.	MIDNIGHT HOUR	WILSON PICKETT	1965
31.	PROUD MARY	CREEDENCE CLEARWATER	1969
32.	YESTERDAY	THE BEATLES	1965
33.	I FALL TO PIECES	PATSY CLINE	1961

41.	DOWNTOWN	PETULA CLARK	1965
42.	CRIMSON & CLOVER	TOMMY JAMES/SHONDELLS	1969
43.	HELLO DOLLY	LOUIS ARMSTRONG	1964
44.	PENNY LANE	THE BEATLES	1967
45.	HARPER VALLEY P.T.A.	JEANNIE C. RILEY	1968
46.	YOU'VE LOST THAT LOVIN' FEELING	THE RIGHTEOUS BROS.	1965
47.	WALK DON'T RUN	THE VENTURES	1960
48.	BACK IN MY ARMS AGAIN	THE SUPREMES	1966
49.	BAD MOON RISING	CREEDENCE CLEARWATER	1969
50.	THE MOUNTAINS HIGH	DICK & DEEDEE	1961
51.	MY CUP RUNNETH OVER	ED AMES	1967
52.	SUNNY	BOBBY HEBB	1966
53.	LAST KISS	J. FRANK WILSON	1964
54.	CRYIN'	ROY ORBISON	1961
55.	GET OFF MY CLOUD	THE ROLLING STONES	1965
56.	THE END OF THE WORLD	SKEETER DAVIS	1963
57.	REACH OUT I'LL BE THERE	THE FOUR TOPS	1966
58.	BALLAD OF BONNIE & CLYDE	GEORGIE FAME	1968
59.	LAY LADY LAY	BOB DYLAN	1969
60.	ON A CAROUSEL	THE HOLLIES	1967
61.	JOHNNY ANGEL	SHELLY FABRES	1962
62.	GREEN TAMBOURINE	THE LEMON PIPERS	1968
63.	FOR WHAT IT'S WORTH	BUFFALO SPRINGFIELD	1967
64.	A HARD DAY'S NIGHT	THE BEATLES	1964
65.	THE LION SLEEPS TONIGHT	THE TOKENS	1962
66.	LITTLE WOMAN	BOBBY SHERMAN	1969
67.	I WILL FOLLOW HIM	PEGGY MARCH	1963
68.	SLIP AWAY	CLARENCE CARTER	1968
69.	96 TEARS	? AND THE MYSTERIANS	1966
70.	ODE TO BILLY JOE	BOBBIE GENTRY	1967
71.	RUNAWAY	DEL SHANNON	1961
72.	SUNSHINE SUPERMAN	DONOVAN	1966
73.	THIS DIAMOND RING	GARY LEWIS & PLAYBOYS	1965

At the end of the 1960s, KAKC aired the countdown of Tulsa's top 100 songs of the decade. Listeners could write in and get this official listing of the songs. "Light My Fire," released in 1967, was the decade's No. 1 song, according to this survey. However, a few months later, KAKC aired another top-songs-of-the-1960s show, based on the national charts, with the Beatles' "Hey Jude" taking the top spot. (Courtesy of the author.)

Randy Brown, a.k.a. Bob Scott, of KAKC designed this 1971 version of the KAKC survey, now simply called the *97/KAKC Thirty*. Right, the week before Christmas 1971 lists Melanie's biggest hit, "Brand New Key," as No. 1. What would become one of the biggest songs of the coming year, Don McLean's iconic "American Pie," is scaling the charts in leaps and bounds. Below, the back of a summer 1972 survey promotes an upcoming Leon Russell show. With the increasing importance of albums, the survey began listing Tulsa's favorite LPs. Here, the Rolling Stones' *Exile On Main Street* tops that chart. (Both, courtesy of Wayne McCombs.)

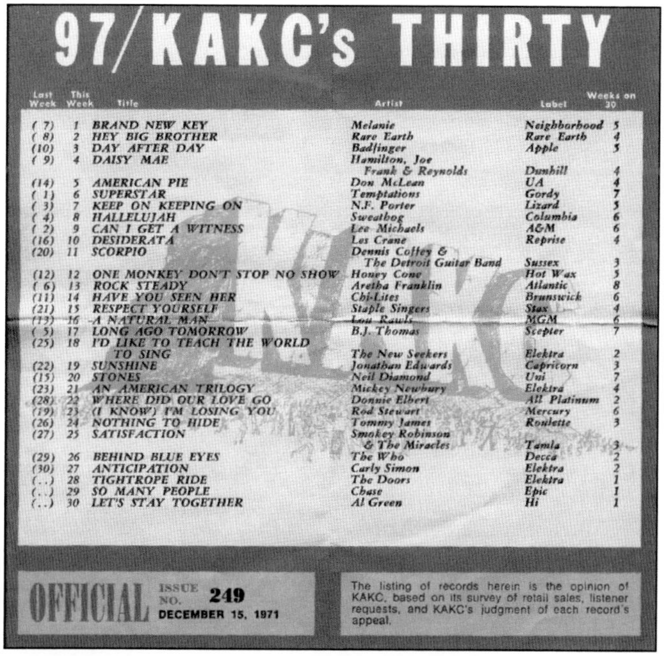

97/KAKC's THIRTY

Last Week	This Week	Title	Artist	Label	Weeks on 30
(7)	1	BRAND NEW KEY	Melanie	Neighborhood	5
(8)	2	HEY BIG BROTHER	Rare Earth	Rare Earth	4
(10)	3	DAY AFTER DAY	Badfinger	Apple	5
(9)	4	DAISY MAE	Hamilton, Joe Frank & Reynolds	Dunhill	4
(14)	5	AMERICAN PIE	Don McLean	UA	4
(1)	6	SUPERSTAR	Temptations	Gordy	7
(3)	7	KEEP ON KEEPING ON	N.F. Porter	Lizard	5
(4)	8	HALLELUJAH	Sweathog	Columbia	6
(2)	9	CAN I GET A WITNESS	Lee Michaels	A&M	6
(16)	10	DESIDERATA	Les Crane	Reprise	4
(20)	11	SCORPIO	Dennis Coffey & The Detroit Guitar Band	Sussex	3
(12)	12	ONE MONKEY DON'T STOP NO SHOW	Honey Cone	Hot Wax	5
(6)	13	ROCK STEADY	Aretha Franklin	Atlantic	8
(11)	14	HAVE YOU SEEN HER	Chi-Lites	Brunswick	6
(21)	15	RESPECT YOURSELF	Staple Singers	Stax	4
(13)	16	A NATURAL MAN	Lou Rawls	MGM	6
(5)	17	LONG AGO TOMORROW	B.J. Thomas	Scepter	7
(25)	18	I'D LIKE TO TEACH THE WORLD TO SING	The New Seekers	Elektra	2
(22)	19	SUNSHINE	Jonathan Edwards	Capricorn	3
(15)	20	STONES	Neil Diamond	Uni	7
(23)	21	AN AMERICAN TRILOGY	Mickey Newbury	Elektra	4
(28)	22	WHERE DID OUR LOVE GO	Donnie Elbert	All Platinum	2
(19)	23	(I KNOW) I'M LOSING YOU	Rod Stewart	Mercury	6
(26)	24	NOTHING TO HIDE	Tommy James	Roulette	3
(27)	25	SATISFACTION	Smokey Robinson & The Miracles	Tamla	3
(29)	26	BEHIND BLUE EYES	The Who	Decca	2
(30)	27	ANTICIPATION	Carly Simon	Elektra	2
(..)	28	TIGHTROPE RIDE	The Doors	Elektra	1
(..)	29	SO MANY PEOPLE	Chase	Epic	1
(..)	30	LET'S STAY TOGETHER	Al Green	Hi	1

OFFICIAL ISSUE NO. 249 DECEMBER 15, 1971

The listing of records herein is the opinion of KAKC, based on its survey of retail sales, listener requests, and KAKC's judgment of each record's appeal.

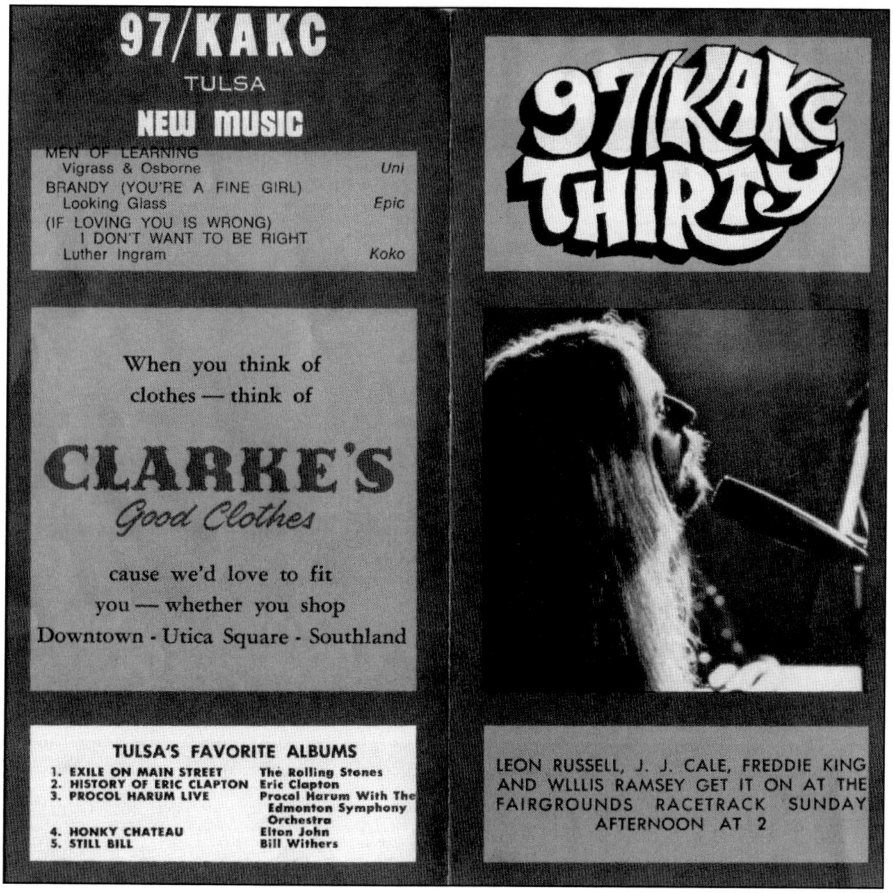

97/KAKC
TULSA
NEW MUSIC

MEN OF LEARNING
Vigrass & Osborne — Uni
BRANDY (YOU'RE A FINE GIRL)
Looking Glass — Epic
(IF LOVING YOU IS WRONG) I DON'T WANT TO BE RIGHT
Luther Ingram — Koko

When you think of clothes — think of
CLARKE'S
Good Clothes
cause we'd love to fit you — whether you shop
Downtown - Utica Square - Southland

TULSA'S FAVORITE ALBUMS

1. EXILE ON MAIN STREET — The Rolling Stones
2. HISTORY OF ERIC CLAPTON — Eric Clapton
3. PROCOL HARUM LIVE — Procol Harum With The Edmonton Symphony Orchestra
4. HONKY CHATEAU — Elton John
5. STILL BILL — Bill Withers

97/KAKC THIRTY

LEON RUSSELL, J. J. CALE, FREDDIE KING AND WLLLIS RAMSEY GET IT ON AT THE FAIRGROUNDS RACETRACK SUNDAY AFTERNOON AT 2

97AM kakc FM93

THE MUSIC IN TULSA

LAST WEEK	THIS WEEK			
(5)	1	NATURAL HIGH	Bloodstone	London
(1)	2	BAD, BAD LEROY BROWN	Jim Croce	ABC
(13)	3	UNEASY RIDER	Charlie Daniels	Kama Sutra
(2)	4	GET DOWN	Gilbert O'Sullivan	Mam
(15)	5	BROTHER LOUIE	Stories	Kama Sutra
(9)	6	MISDEMEANOR	Foster Sylvers	MGM
(8)	7	LIVE AND LET DIE	Wings	Apple
(10)	8	TOUCH ME IN THE MORNING	Diana Ross	Motown
(11)	9	FEELIN' STRONGER EVERY DAY	Chicago	Columbia
(4)	10	MONEY	Pink Floyd	Harvest
(3)	11	DIAMOND GIRL	Seals & Crofts	WB
(6)	12	BOOGIE WOOGIE BUGLE BOY	Bette Midler	Atlantic
(14)	13	SMOKE ON THE WATER	Deep Purple	WB
(17)	14	LORD, MR. FORD	Jerry Reed	RCA
(18)	15	DELTA DAWN	Helen Reddy	Capitol
(21)	16	ROLL OVER BEETHOVEN	Electric Light Orchestra	UA
(12)	17	SO VERY HARD TO GO	Tower Of Power	WB
(22)	18	HOW CAN I TELL HER	Lobo	Big Tree
(25)	19	YOUNG LOVE/A MILLION TO ONE	Donny Osmond	MGM
(7)	20	BACK WHEN MY HAIR WAS SHORT	Gunhill Road	Kama Sutra
(24)	21	CLOUDS	David Gates	Elektra
(28)	22	LET'S GET IT ON	Marvin Gaye	Tamla
(16)	23	THE MORNING AFTER	Maureen McGovern	20th Century
(30)	24	GYPSY MAN	War	UA
(27)	25	I BELIEVE IN YOU	Johnnie Taylor	Stax
(20)	26	DADDY COULD SWEAR, I DECLARE	Gladys Knight & The Pips	Soul
(19)	27	BEHIND CLOSED DOORS	Charlie Rich	Epic
(--)	28	SAY, HAS ANYBODY SEEN MY SWEET GYPSY ROSE	Dawn	Bell
(--)	29	HALF-BREED	Cher	MCA
(--)	30	MY MARIA	B.W. Stevenson	RCA

Tulsa's trippiest taxi: SCOOTER B. SEGRAVES...drivin' you home, 3 til 6.

This 1973 version of the KAKC record survey reflects the changing landscape of music and radio. On the front, both 97AM and FM93 appear at the top of the survey because, at that time, KAKC-AM's Top 40 programming could also be heard on 93FM (92.9) KAKC-FM in the evenings. Compared to KAKC's surveys of previous years, which were always of high quality in look and design, this one is particularly plain. Jim Croce's "Bad, Bad Leroy Brown," one of 1973's biggest hits, was at No. 2, behind "Natural High" by Bloodstone. Below, on the back, the Rockin' 97 solicits listener feedback on what kind of prizes people would like to win. Note that this survey not only lists Tulsa's top albums, but also Tulsa's top tapes (eight-tracks). (Both, courtesy of Wayne McCombs.)

KAKC THE BIG 97

THE ALBUMS

1. CHICAGO VI
2. FOREIGNER — Cat Stevens
3. FRESH — Sly & The Family Stone
4. LEON LIVE — Leon Russell
5. PASSION PLAY — Jethro Tull

THE LATEST

THE HURT — Cat Stevens
ARE YOU MAN ENOUGH — Four Tops
ANGEL — Aretha Franklin

The Rockin' 97 wants to know what you want to win.

We've given away thousands of dollars in cash...cars... albums...trips...boats... groceries...and more.

But we don't know what YOU want most:

Mail us a postcard (no letters, please) saying exactly what you would like to win, regardless of the price.

Be sure to include your name, age, address, and phone number.

Mail to: PRIZE
KAKC, Box 970

THE TAPES

1. CHICAGO VI
2. FOREIGNER — Cat Stevens
3. FRESH — Sly & The Family Stone
4. LEON LIVE — Leon Russell
5. PASSION PLAY — Jethro Tull

OFFICIAL

ISSUE NO. 334 - AUGUST 1, 1973
The listing of records herein is the opinion of KAKC, based on its survey of retail sales, listener requests, juke box plays, and KAKC's judgment of each record's appeal.

Six

Passing into Legend

S. Carl Mark sold KAKC-AM970 to Salem Communications in 1980. For a few years, the new company retained the KAKC call letters for its gospel programming, but dropped them in 1984 to become KCFO-AM.

But the iconic call sign was resurrected in 1986 by Clear Channel for their AM1300 station. At first, with the help of Tulsa radio broadcaster and musician John Henry, there was talk of trying to recapture the old KAKC magic. But it was not to be. The station did run a syndicated oldies format for a time, with John Henry doing a live daily show, but the station never made a dent in the Tulsa ratings. After numerous format changes, KAKC-AM1300 eventually became part of the ESPN Radio Network.

Tulsa radio listeners missed their best chance to celebrate KAKC's Top 40 heritage. During the 1980s and 1990s especially, oldies-formatted stations flourished in cities around the country. Many of them, like 92.5 KOMA in Oklahoma City and K-EARTH 101 in Los Angeles, featured marquee deejays from their cities' Top 40 pasts. These stations were even made to sound like the ones listeners grew up with. However, Tulsa's oldies station, KOOL 106.1 (KQLL) never quite captured the feel of Tulsa's Top 40 heritage, and none of the KAKC deejays came back to work there. In 2009, KOOL 106.1 dropped oldies to become GenX radio, only to change to 106.1 the Twister with a country format in 2012.

But KAKC has been remembered in other ways. In 2004, Dick Schmitz was honored as a Tulsa Radio Icon by the Tulsa Press Club, an honor Scooter Segraves also received one year later. Schmitz also was also voted into the Oklahoma Association of Broadcasters Hall of Fame in 2005. Clayton Vaughn received that honor in 2001 and also received the Tulsa Press Club's Tulsa TV Icon award. Tulsa historian Jack Frank featured KAKC in his *Tulsa History Series* of video documentaries, in the show entitled "Stuff That's Gone." Tulsa author and music historian John Wooley spotlighted the early KAKC in his award-winning *Rock Of Ages*, a series in the *Tulsa World* about the early days of rock and roll in the city.

In September 2010, KWGS 89.5 aired the award-winning documentary, "Tulsa's Top 40 Legend, KAKC." The following year, the exhibit, The Big 97: Tulsa's KAKC Radio, opened at the Tulsa Historical Society, sparking renewed interest in the station with fans as well as the media. It ran through 2012 and spawned two KAKC deejay reunions.

In the 1980s, after S. Carl Mark sold the station to Salem Communications, KAKC-AM970 was gospel. In a sense, the station had come full-circle, since it had been the domain of radio preachers in its pre–rock and roll years. When Salem changed the call letters of AM970 to KCFO in 1984, the KAKC call sign was not dormant in the Tulsa market for long. Realizing the nostalgic value, in 1986, Clear Channel picked up the iconic call letters for their station on AM1300. This is the logo the station used when it carried a live rock-and-roll show hosted by John Henry and a satellite oldies format the rest of the day. (Courtesy of Wayne McCombs.)

There was one man who tried single-handedly to keep KAKC's memory alive in Tulsa radio: John Henry. For 25 years, Henry hosted various radio shows and worked at several different Tulsa stations, including KELI 1430, KGTO AM1050, KMOD 97.5, KAKC-AM1300, and KOOL 106.1. He is probably best known for his specialty show, *Saturday Bandstand*, heard on various Tulsa stations through the years. It featured early rock and roll, blues, and R&B. In his big, booming voice, John told the stories behind the songs and spotlighted Oklahoma connections to the music. A musician himself, Henry fronted a rock-and-roll revival band called the Bopcats. Regardless of the station he was on, Henry often mentioned the early KAKC and the influence it had on him. This is a tribute poster featuring "Rockin' " John Henry through the years. Henry died in 2004 and posthumously received the Tulsa Radio Icon award from the Tulsa Press Club. He is also a member of the Rockabilly Hall of Fame. (Courtesy of Jill Henry-Riley.)

The Big 97: Tulsa's KAKC Radio exhibit was a partnership between the Tulsa Historical Society and Pubic Radio 89.5 KWGS. It opened in June 2011 with a reception for THS members. Above is the cool, retro invitation that was sent to museum members. The display, pictured below, featured KAKC photographs and memorabilia, 1960s fashions and cultural artifacts, a jukebox filled with 1960s records, and historical commentary about the station from the radio documentary *Tulsa's Top 40 Legend, KAKC,* which aired originally on KWGS 89.5 in September 2010. (Both, courtesy of the Tulsa Historical Society.)

At the opening reception of The Big 97: Tulsa's KAKC Radio, Scooter Segraves autographs copies of the KAKC radio documentary and a Top 50 record survey. In the background, a copy of the *KAKC Solid Gold* album, brought by someone to be signed by the deejays, is visible. Also pictured, from left to right, are Lou Vespasian (wearing glasses), Wayne McCombs, and Roy Payton. (Courtesy of Sandra Wiley.)

Maggie Brown, the Tulsa Historical Society's exhibits and education manager, designed the well-received KAKC exhibit. In this image, she stands beside the giant turquoise and cream transistor radio designed and built for the display. This c. 1960-style transistor (with its dial turned to AM 970, the Big 97) played original KAKC audio as people browsed the exhibit. In addition to the history of KAKC, the show portrays the life of a Tulsa teenager during the 1960s and 1970s. "Examples of fashions, household items, and photos of teens and their daily activities depict the culture of the times," says Brown. (Left, courtesy of Becky Leedy; below, courtesy of Nancy Schallner.)

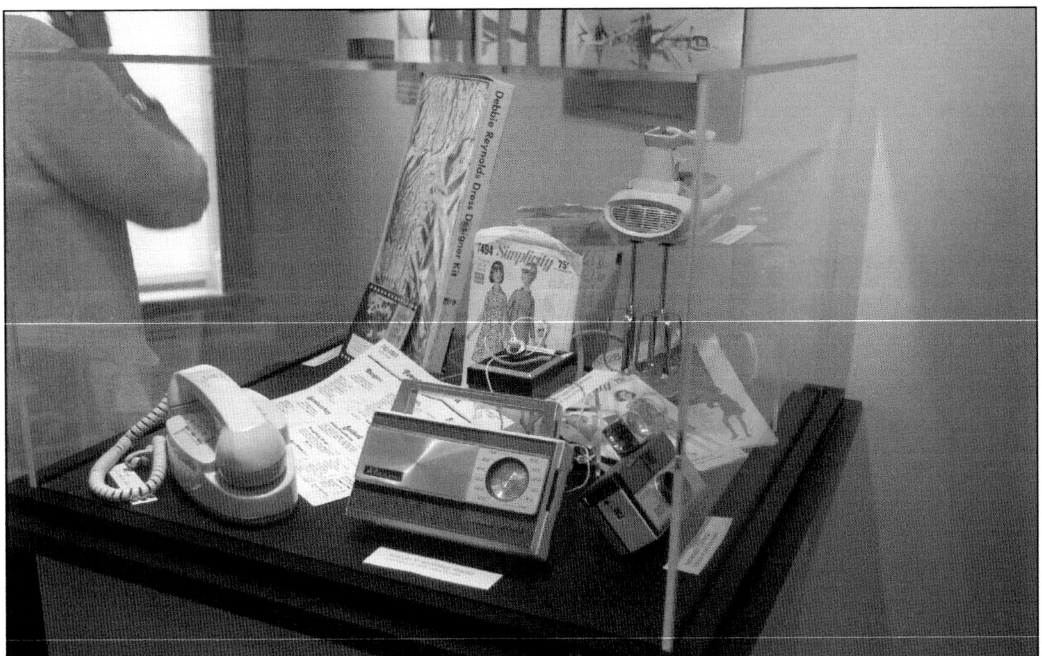

At the exhibit's opening, Scooter Segraves poses next to an early 1960s photograph of himself working at the KAKC control board. Of the attention generated by the display, Segraves says, " I was playing songs on the radio and having fun, and these people are kind enough to say 'I remembered you and I enjoyed you' 40 and 50 years later. That's pretty nice stuff." (Courtesy of the author.)

As part of the opening reception, there was a panel discussion by former KAKC personnel. It was standing-room only as each former Big 97 staffer took their turn telling stories and answering questions. Seen here awaiting their turn at the microphone are, from left to right, Dick Schmitz, Clayton Vaughn, Mike McCarthy, and Steve Suttle. (Courtesy of Sandra Wiley.)

As the closing of the exhibit drew near, the Tulsa Historical Society had another party—a sock hop with the KAKC deejays. Here, the former KAKC airmen pose for a photograph. They are, from left to right, Steve Suttle, Harry Wilson, Dick Schmitz, Clayton Vaughn, Denver Foxx, Scooter Segraves, Gary "Ono" Stevens, Mike McCarthy, and John Durkee. (Courtesy of Mary Alice (Mark) Alexander.)

At the sock hop, Dick Schmitz (left), Clayton Vaughn (center), and Harry Wilson (right) pose for a picture. These three men, along with Scooter Segraves, were the nucleus of the on-air staff at the New KAKC in the late 1950s and early 1960s. (Courtesy of Clayton Vaughn.)

The sock hop featured oldies music and twist and hula hoop contests hosted by the KAKC deejays. Pictured with one of the hula hoops are Scooter Segraves and Janet Haggard. (Courtesy of Michael Dethrow.)

The last great KAKC air staff was the mid-1970s Rockin' 97 team. Posing at the KAKC Sock Hop in July 2012, they are, from left to right, Denver Foxx, Scooter Segraves, Gary Stevens, and Mike McCarthy. Charlie Derek, who also worked with this group, is not pictured. (Courtesy of Frank and Betty Christel.)

A special guest at both exhibit parties was Mary Alice (Mark) Alexander, daughter of S. Carl Mark, KAKC's owner. Alexander, who flew in from Boston, spoke at the panel discussion, telling the crowd what it was like having KAKC as the family business. She also told about working there in the summer of 1970 and being the voice on commercials for the teen shop at Miss Jackson's while she was in college. She is pictured in 2012 viewing the KAKC exhibit. (Courtesy of Mary Alice (Mark) Alexander.)

S. Carl Mark's son Jon Mark also attended the KAKC sock hop. Mark (left), pictured with Dick Schmitz, was vice president and assistant general manager of KAKC-AM970 and KAKC-FM 92.9 from 1975 to 1980. Mark recalls that, when they were launching KBEZ 92.9 as a beautiful music station, they sought call letters with *EZ* in them. The two choices were KQEZ and KBEZ; they chose KBEZ because they felt KQEZ might lead to the unflattering nickname "Queasy." (Courtesy of Mary Alice (Mark) Alexander.)

On April 12, 2012, KAKC alum Bob Brown was inducted into the University of Tulsa Communication Hall Of Fame. Brown graduated from TU with a journalism degree in 1968 while working in Tulsa television. Beginning in 1980, he spent 30 years as a correspondent on *20/20* for ABC News. Pictured at Brown's Hall of Fame reception are, from left to right, Steve Clem, Bob Brown, and Bob Losure (another KAKC alumni). (Courtesy of Wayne McCombs.)

In November 2009, Scooter Segraves drove in from Arkansas to the KWGS studios on the University of Tulsa campus to be interviewed for the radio documentary, *Tulsa's Top 40 Legend, KAKC*. Segraves (left) is pictured with Steve Clem, the documentary's writer/producer (and author of this book) immediately following a "Goldie's Patio Grill" break. (Courtesy of P. Casey Morgan.)